# THE SPIRIT BEHIND THE VOICE

CONNOR COURT PUBLISHING PTY LTD
PO Box 7257
Redland Bay QLD 4165
sales@connorcourt.com
www.connorcourt.com

ISBN: 9781922815613

The cover of the book is a drawing by **Joris Van der Mijnsbrugge**, a Belgian sculptor who died in 2003. The imaginative and expressive style of his work is admired widely and contributed to his international reputation. The figurines at the top of the drawing could represent the members of the "Voice" who feed 'advice' to the government, which then proceeds to divide the Australian polity by throwing arrows at it. On the right of the drawing is a dog, who appears to be treated better than the Australian population. Used with permission.

Cover design by Maria Giordano

Printed in Australia

# THE SPIRIT BEHIND THE VOICE

## The Religious Dimension of the "Voice" Proposal

Gabriël Moens AM

Emeritus Professor of Law, The University of Queensland

Augusto Zimmermann

Head and Professor of Law, Sheridan Institute of Higher Education

Connor Court Publishing

# TABLE OF CONTENTS

# FOREWORD

## Bess Nungarrayi Price AM [*]

My father was born in 1914 in Southern Warlpiri country. He saw kardiya (white men) for the first time when he was around 12 years old. My mother, born in 1929, was an infant when she first saw them. When he was 14 Dad had to run far to the west with other refugees to avoid the killing that began on Coniston Station after the murder of a kardiya by one of our people, Kamalyarrpa Japanangka. Between 70 and 100 Warlpiri, Anmatyerr and Kaytetye men, women and children were killed by the avenging police party which included Aboriginal men. When the respected and trusted Lutheran missionary, Friedrich Albrecht, caught up with the refugees, they told him that they would have handed over the killer of if they'd been asked. Kamalyarrpa survived until 1959. All who had died in his place were innocent.

Once the killing had stopped Dad was happy to work for kardiya on the stations. He convinced his own father that the troubles were over and the kardiya could then be trusted. He understood that not all kardiya were dangerous and bad. Then in 1942 he was arrested by a policeman led to him and his relatives by an Aboriginal tracker. They, and several others, were chained and walked naked and barefoot behind camels, to what was to become the Stuart Highway, then trucked to Alice Springs to be locked up. He thought he had been arrested for spearing goats on Mt Doreen

[*] Bess Nungarrayi Price AM is an Aboriginal Australian activist, artist and politician. She was an elected member of the Northern Territory Legislative Assembly from 2012 to 2016, holding positions as minister for community services, local government and housing. Price's daughter, Jacinta Nampijinpa Price, is a Senator for the Northern Territory and the Shadow Minister for Indigenous Affairs.

Station but actually he and the others were being recruited to labour for the Army for 5 shillings a week when a skilled kardiya labourer could earn twenty times as much. He worked for the Army until the end of the war. He was always proud that he had helped to build much of the infrastructure of Alice Springs. He then settled at Yuendumu, set up in 1946, and married my mother.

There he met, worked for and befriended the Baptist minister, Tom Fleming. Tom was a small and compassionate man but tough minded and determined. He had survived imprisonment in Changi and prison camps on Borneo. He didn't set out to destroy our culture but to add to it. He risked his life to stop violence, striding between groups of armed Warlpiri men preparing to attack each other and shaming them into putting down their weapons and walking away. He saved lives. Dad taught Tom Warlpiri and, with many other men his age, helped to build the church at Yuendumu as well as a men's museum to house traditional sacred objects. He was a leading law man by then, many of the younger men at Yuendumu have told me that he had taught and supported them through their initiation.

He and many other ritual leaders, both men and women, also called themselves Christian. In the 1980's a strange new ritual was brought to our community from the North West. It involved forcing men and women to sit for hours in the sun, then to be locked up at night and to be relieved of their money and valuables. My parents would have none of it. It was not traditional, and they thought it strange and oppressive. They retreated to the church and asked the missionary to protect them from it. They believed that we could be both – Christian and Warlpiri – loyal to our traditions, the ones worth keeping but replacing those not worth keeping with the teachings of Christ. They were trying to give our old ways a New Testament, a better way of living while keeping our identity.

Things have changed since then. Naturally those who control the national debate are those people of indigenous descent who speak English and are well educated kardiya way. They have access to the media and politicians and are the loudest in their criticism of governments and kardiya in general. They criticise the old missionaries, But they don't live by the Old Law and never have. They romanticise it, creating what I call a Disneyland version. They never talk about the downside, the acceptance of violence as a way to settle conflicts, the misogyny and acceptance of violence against women, the forcing of young girls into marriage with old men, the belief in sorcery. These old ways still cause a lot of problems, like continued violence against women, family feuding and the humbugging that forces so many to give their money to addicted kin for grog and gambling. All of these things come from the culture we were taught as children. The so called First Nations Leaders tell us that all of these things are caused by kardiya, by racism and colonisation. They have made everything worse, but all of these problems come from our own culture. The 'leaders' call any kardiya racist if they say this and they put great effort into 'cancelling' Aboriginal people like me who want the truth to be known.

In 2009, I was appointed as the inaugural chair of the NT government's indigenous Affairs Advisory Council by then Deputy Chief Minister Marion Scrymgour. She resigned from the government the same day. Our council then reported to Minister Alison Anderson who soon after resigned as well. We then reported to Minister Malarndirri McCarthy. Our council was widely representative of men and women from all over the NT, from both the urban, English speaking and remote traditional language speaking Aboriginal population. Although we reported to three Aboriginal women Labor Ministers, I came to feel that we were being effectively ignored by the Labor government. All of our efforts seemed to be in vain.

It was that experience that led me to join the Country Liberal Party to be elected to represent the huge electorate of Stuart and to serve as a Minister, the only woman in cabinet at the time, in our nation's first government to be led by an Indigenous Australian, Adam Giles. I took the place of Alison Anderson in the cabinet after she had resigned from that government as well. She then went on to campaign against me and my daughter in subsequent elections. Marion Scrymgour is now member for the Federal seat of Lingiari and Malarndirri McCarthy is now Labor Senator for the NT. Both, vigorously campaign for the Voice to Parliament. My joining the CLP has since made me anathema to the Labor party. They do think that they own us and can't tolerate our dissenting from their narrative. And they don't forget.

My family was denied royalties that we were entitled to by the Central Land Council. My father's role as a senior traditional owner for the country and Dreamings involved were simply denied. When we made a formal complaint, we were denied the most basic natural justice. We have witnessed violence at CLC convened meetings. They don't hesitate to use intimidation and manipulation to achieve their goals. We are at their mercy. I was told to my face by a white CLC staff member; "I am a lawyer. I can tell you that you can't win". But I have not given up.

Too many Aboriginal organisations are run as family fiefdoms with jobs and benefits distributed on the basis of kinship or political loyalties rather than need. A close relative of mine was told that, despite being qualified for a job with one of them, he would not be offered one because he was related to me. Labor governments are no better. I applied for a job with the Health Department that I am eminently qualified for. It is work that I have done voluntarily for decades. The Aboriginal manager of the unit concerned told me that she wanted me on board but there were "problems up stairs". I applied in November of 2021. I have still not received a formal acknowledgement of that application. A woman known to me was given the job within two weeks of applying. Their nefarious, 'culturally appropriate' practices would be enshrined in our constitution if the Voice was passed by the voters.

The Voice advocates are polite and well-mannered in the light of day, but many are offensive and aggressive in the shadows. My daughter, Senator Nampijinpa Price, and I have been threatened with death several times. In the NT we women are used to that. We are routinely vilified in obscene, racist and misogynist terms simply because we disagree with the Left's narrative. Get Up sends young Aboriginal women, mostly from Down South to campaign against us in elections in favour of kardiya who have done nothing for us. We have been ignored or defamed by the mainstream media. I was awarded with an Australia Medal on Australia Day this year. I was contacted by commercial media from all over the country, but I have not been contacted once by the ABC, even in my own town of Alice Springs. The Green/Left wish we didn't exist. We have a different point of view that they don't want to be heard.

I am deeply disappointed by the churches who have accepted this aggressive wokeness and allowed themselves to become naïve virtue signallers rather than moral guardians and teachers. My people are crying out for moral guidance. Instead, they are being told that their culture, however defined by the Left of politics, is always right. Our culture should be critically analysed and improved like any other. We are not all just 'Victims' who can't help ourselves and our culture is faultless. Kardiya are told to do away with their traditional religion. The old missionaries are condemned. Yet we, in the NT, can tell as soon as an older Aboriginal person from a remote community speaks, that they were taught by missionaries. They were taught to properly speak, read and write English, while speaking, reading and writing their own first languages. It was missionaries who first started teaching in both languages, in the case of Ntaria/Hermannsburg, a century before governments. Now our kids are not taught to speak English properly let alone read and write it, in the name of preserving a culture and languages that are fast disappearing anyway. That is why they don't want to go to school. Governments need to learn from the missionaries not from their enemies.

The Voice is being promoted by those who are living off our peoples' miseries. They are the educated, confident ones who constantly blame kardiya for our problems and do all they can to keep voices like mine unheard. They are not interested in truth telling; they are interested in imposing their own narrative as the new Gospel. Now anybody can claim to be 'First Nations' without challenge. My husband of 44 years, the father of my daughter and tens of thousands of other Australians of all ethnicities who have had children with Aboriginal people, would not be able to vote for a Voice representative or stand for election because they don't 'identify'. They would have no say in what is good for the welfare of their loved ones and their descendants. Yet anybody who ticks a box on a government form proclaiming themselves, unchallenged, as 'indigenous' will be able to. If the Voice gets up, people who have no relevant lived experience, no knowledge of traditional culture or history and, for too many, no actual descent from our old people, will be able to advise government on what is good and right for our family and our descendants.

I will be voting NO and I urge all Australians with a conscience, whatever their religion, to do the same. I am sick of burying our children, seeing education denied to them, seeing them incarcerated, living in dire poverty and taken from families that don't know how to care for them. We want real solutions and decision makers willing to listen to all of us, whatever our politics and the languages we speak. We need open ears not a constitutionally embedded, bureaucratised, highly selective Voice set up and run by those who have controlled the narrative and the funds for decades while everything got worse for us.

# CONTRIBUTORS

**Peter Barnes** is a Presbyterian pastor who lives in Sydney.

**Gabriël Moens AM** is Emeritus Professor of Law at the University of Queensland.

**Augusto Zimmermann** is Head and Professor of Law at Sheridan Institute of Higher Education and a former member of the Law Reform Commission of Western Australia.

**Bob Gregory** is a retired Pastor and Christian School Principal.

**Mark Powell** is the Teaching Elder at Cornerstone Presbyterian Community Church in Hobart.

**Neil Johnson** is Head of News and Current Affairs at Vision Christian Media.

**Julie Sladden** is a medical doctor, founding director of Australians for Science and Freedom, and Local Government Councillor for the West Tamar in Tasmania.

**Thomas Eglinton** is a Pastor at Smithfield Baptist Church, a Reformed Baptist church located in Sydney's South West.

**Dave Pellowe** is the director of Church And State Ministries, and presenter of The Church And State Show, which airs weekly on ADH.TV.

**Rocco Loiacono** is a Senior Lecturer in Law, Curtin University.

**Shimon Cowen** is an Australian rabbi and academic. He is Director of the Institute for Judaism and Civilization in Melbourne, Australia.

**John Fleming** is an author and academic, specialising in medical ethics, political philosophy and public policy.

**David Daintree** is director of the Christopher Dawson Centre for Cultural Studies in Tasmania. He served as President of Campion College from 2008 to 2012.

**Matthew Littlefield** is the pastor of New Beith Baptist Church. He is an ordained Minister in the Baptist Union of Queensland.

**Paul Collits** is a freelance writer and independent researcher. He has taught at tertiary level in three different disciplines - politics, geography and planning and business studies.

**Minny Rozario** is an independent journalist, final year Juris Doctor student and national ministry worker. She worked for seven years in remote Indigenous communities doing scripture-based annual camps.

**James Allan** is the Garrick Professor of Law at the University of Queensland.

# INTRODUCTION: THE RELIGIOUS DIMENSION OF THE "VOICE" PROPOSAL

**Gabriël A. Moens* and Augusto Zimmermann****

When surfing the Internet, we came across a number of commentaries, which estimated that since March 2020 several hundreds of thousands of scholarly or journalistic pieces have been published about the COVID-19 pandemic, either online or in hard copy. We expect that since July 2022 – not much longer than one year ago – the total number of articles of the Voice might well compete with the record number of COVID-19 articles for the title of the most written about topic of the decade. Indeed, the voluminous literature on the Voice is staggeringly unbelievable. Hence, it is necessary to explain why we regard this book, *The Spirit of the Voice: The Religious Dimension of the "Voice" Proposal,* as making an original contribution to the debate on the proposed entrenchment of the Voice in the Constitution.

To some extent, it is surprising that the Voice generated such a huge output of commentaries. Unlike COVID-19, very few Australians actually know anything at all about the proposal to entrench this "consultative body" in the Constitution. This is because the Federal government, the initiator of the referendum to be held later in 2023, has released but scant details of this controversial amendment of the Constitution, which would

* Gabriël A. Moens is an Emeritus Professor of Law at the University of Queensland.

** Augusto Zimmermann is Head and Professor of Law at Sheridan Institute of Higher Education and a former commissioner with the Law Reform Commission of Western Australia have its own Chapter in the nation's founding document. If the referendum were to be successful, details would have to be worked out by the Parliament, now dominated by the Labor Party, and the implications of the 'modest' proposal – a word used by the Prime Minister, Anthony Albanese – would be revealed to Australia's unsuspecting citizens.

The Voice is the current Labor government's response to the recommendations made by an Aboriginal National Constitutional Convention held in 2017 near Uluru, which resulted in the release of a pamphlet, the *Uluru Statement from the Heart*. There is no denying the reality that this Statement galvanised a movement to amend the Australian Constitution. It invites people to walk with Aboriginals and Torres Strait Islander people "in a movement of the Australian people for a better future."[1]

This Statement is but one part of a complex set of initiatives to increase the overall participation of Indigenous people in the governance of Australia. For example, the South Australian government and the Victorian government have already legislated for a State Voice. The government of the Australian Capital Territory also has an Indigenous representative body.

In Queensland, on May 10, the state Parliament, with the support of the Opposition and the Greens adopted the *Path to Treaty Act* 2023. Although the papers and opinion pages are saturated with stories about 'The Voice' and First Nations' claims to sovereignty over Australia, there has been little discussion of this potentially divisive legislative development.[2] While it is not a surprise that

1 The Uluru Statement from the Heart is available at: https://ulurustatemdev.wpengine.com/wp-content/uploads/2022/01/UluruStatementfromtheHeartPLAINTEXT.pdf.

2 Gabriël Moens, 'Queensland Liberal-Nationals' Impotence on Full Display With Support for Treaty Bill', *The Epoch Times*, June 5, 2023, at https://www.theepochtimes.com/queenslands-treaty-bill-puts-impotence-of-liberal-nationals-on-full-display_5314732.html.

the long-serving Queensland Labor government has used its majority to steamroll this legislation through Parliament, it is surprising that the Opposition sheepishly supported it, effectively championing and applauding Labor's social engineering agenda. The Queensland Opposition Leader, David Crisafulli, insists that he will "absolutely not" roll back Indigenous treaty legislation if he becomes premier next year, even if there is intense pressure from his party to overturn the *Path to Treaty Act*. However, it has since been reported that he intends to vote 'No' in the referendum., claiming 'he is concerned about the 'risks' involved in enshrining the Voice in the constitution.'[3]

The main purposes of the Queensland legislation are to establish the *First Nations Treaty Institute*. This Institute will "develop and provide a framework for Aboriginal peoples, Torres Strait Islander peoples and the State to enter into treaty negotiations; and support Aboriginal peoples and Torres Strait Islander peoples to participate in treaty negotiations."[4] In addition, the legislation provides for the establishment of a Truth-telling and Healing Inquiry to inquire into and report on "the impacts of colonisation on Aboriginal peoples." The Truth-telling Inquiry will be able to arrogate to itself inquisition-style powers to rewrite the history of Queensland.

Similarly, the Uluru Statement from the Heart proposes the establishment of an Indigenous Voice to the federal parliament, and the Makarrata Commission to supervise a process of agreement-making with Australian governments and oversee a process of truth-telling about Australia's history and colonisation.

On 30 July 2022, Prime Minister, Anthony Albanese, used an address at the *Indigenous Garma Festival* in the Northern Territory

3 'The Crisafulli Redemption', *The Spectator Australia,* 3 June 2023, 1

4 Section 4, *Path to Treaty Act* 2023

to declare his unqualified support for the Voice and to reveal the referendum question which may be put to the Australian people. The question is: "Do you support an alteration to the Constitution that establishes an Aboriginal and Torres Strait Islander Voice?" The *Constitution Alteration Bill* was approved in the Commonwealth House of Representatives, and was finally endorsed by the Senate on Monday, 19 June, thereby paving the way for a referendum to be held, later in 2023.

Three provisions will be added to the Constitution if the referendum were to succeed: the first would entrench the Voice in the Constitution; the second would allow the Voice to make representations to parliament and the executive government on matters relating to Indigenous Australians. The third proposes to insert, into the Constitution, a new head of legislative power, according to which the parliament shall have power to make laws with respect to the functions and procedures of the Voice.

The Leader of the Nationals Party, David Littleproud, confirmed in November 2022 that his Party would not support the Voice. Similarly, the Liberal Party decided in April 2023 to campaign for a 'No' vote. Consequently, Julian Leeser, who served as Shadow Minister for Indigenous Affairs at the time, relinquished his position because he wants to campaign for a "Yes" vote in favour of the Voice. The Opposition Leader, Peter Dutton, then wisely appointed the indomitable Senator Jacinta Nampijinpa Price to become the Shadow Minister.

Representatives of the "No" campaign argue that the entrenchment of The Voice in the Constitution would repudiate a central tenet of classical liberalism—the idea that all people should be treated equally. Opponents of the Voice also argue that, in locking in an institutionalised Indigenous Voice body, Australia will be embracing governing arrangements that violate the principle of equal treatment of all citizens. They believe that the

Voice will undermine the long-term future of Australia's liberal democracy (which, on any comparative basis, has been one of the world's most successful).

If the Voice were to be entrenched in the Constitution, it would effectively become impossible to remove this body because it could only be terminated in accordance with section 128 of the Constitution, which requires a referendum and a double majority – a majority of electors, and a majority of States. Since 1901, 44 proposals have been put to the people, with only eight (or 18 per cent) succeeding. Section 76 of the Constitution says the High Court has original jurisdiction in any matter "Arising under this Constitution, or involving its interpretation". The *Judiciary Act* confers this jurisdiction. Consequently, the High Court would have the final say on the Voice's role in addressing any matter of alleged Aboriginal interest.

Supporters of the Voice often appeal to the history of unequal treatment suffered by Indigenous people. However, the sweeping claim that Australia's history is one of 'unequal treatment' is misleading at best and false at worst. After all, since World War II, governments around Australia have established hundreds of Aboriginal institutional bodies, which maintain and nurture a burgeoning and expensive Indigenous bureaucracy. Billions of dollars have been pumped into determined, and good faith attempts at closing 'the gap'. In addition, native title and land rights have been fully entrenched in Australia's legal system.

Aboriginal men acquired the right to vote in the 1850s under the constitutions of Victoria, New South Wales, and South Australia, meaning that they had the same right to vote as other male British subjects over the age of 21. Voting rights were then extended to all Indigenous Australians in 1962. Even in the 19th century, some white Australians were hanged for killing Aboriginal and/or Torres Strait Islander people.

Many of the contributors to this volume point out that the government's proposed entrenchment of The Voice in the Constitution will not unite Australia. Instead, it will perpetuate divisiveness and welfare dependency that have negatively impacted members of the Aboriginal community. It will force Australians to see the world through the prism of race and, worse, further divide Australians on the basis of race and ancestry.

Curiously, one of the dimensions of the Voice debate that has not been debated in any depth at all is the religious dimension of the Voice. This book seeks to fill that gap in the literature. Most of the contributors to this volume are priests, pastors and clergymen who focus on the important message in the Bible that God created all people, regardless of their race or gender, in His image.

It is hoped that the reading of this book will provide our readers with information about one of the most relevant, albeit underreported, aspects of the debate on the Voice.

# 1

# THE INDIGENOUS VOICE – A CHRISTIAN CASE FOR VOTING 'NO'

**Peter Barnes***

It is not an unusual experience in life – whether political, cultural, or, for that matter, ecclesiastical – to have a sense of facing one way and rowing in the other. Karl Marx and Friedrich Engels proclaimed: 'Workers of the world unite! You have nothing to lose but your chains.' It turned out that the Marxist chains were more oppressive than monarchical ones. Less drastic in its implications was the decision of one misguided Scottish squatter who imported Scotland's national flower, the thistle, into Australia about 1851, and it soon spread as a noxious weed. We all make misjudgements, and we do so even with noble intentions. There is good reason to consider beforehand whether an Indigenous Voice to parliament might not also prove to be a misjudgement.

* Rev Dr Peter Barnes is a Presbyterian pastor who lives in Sydney, Australia.

## 1. Background

In 2017, the National Constitutional Convention issued what became known as the Uluru Statement from the Heart. It declared that there was a 'sacred link' between the Aboriginal and Torres Strait Islander people and the land, adding that 'This link is the basis of the ownership of the soil, or better, of sovereignty. It has never been ceded or extinguished, and co-exists with the sovereignty of the Crown.'

Noting the high rates of aboriginal incarceration, the Statement claimed: 'This is the torment of our powerlessness.' Hence, 'We call for the establishment of a First Nations Voice enshrined in the Constitution.' Nor is this to be the end of the matter. A Makarrata Commission would be set up to 'supervise a process of agreement-making between governments and First Nations and truth-telling about our history.' At times the writing could be pithy and compelling, even when it was misleading: 'In 1967 we were counted, in 2017 we seek to be heard.'[1]

The Statement should be seen as a package deal:

(a) spiritual understanding of the land;

(b) a First Nations Voice in the Constitution;

(c) a treaty; and

(d) a truth-telling commission.

The Prime Minister, Anthony Albanese, has said that this is simply 'good manners', while Emily Hayes, a Uniting Church minister in Alice Springs, has called it 'one of the most ingenious, gracious, generous and practical documents I have read in this space and one of the most beautifully constructed pieces of literature to come out of Australia.'

1 See Geoffrey Blainey, 'Before we vote, let's get our facts in order', *The Weekend Australian*, 1-2 July, 2023.

## 2. Christian objections

The 'sacred link' with the land sounds spiritual, but that is precisely the problem. The Psalmist declares that the earth is the Lord's and everything in it (Ps.24:1). We all come from one man, and God has appointed the periods and boundaries of our lives here on earth (Acts 17:26). Not all humanity is redeemed, but we are all created as the offspring of God (Acts 17:28) and in the image of God (Gen.1:26-28). In Christ there is neither Greek nor Jew (Gal.3:28), barbarian or Scythian (Col.3:11). To seek to help another people group is one thing, but to entrench a racial divide in the Constitution may prove to be quite another.

## 3. Another layer of bureaucracy

This is an oft-repeated fear, and with good reason. There are three proposed layers: national, regional, and local. The national body is meant to consist of 24 indigenous people; there are meant to be 25-35 regional voices; and any number of local voices. Elected advisory bodies have been set up in the past – four of them since 1973, namely the National Aboriginal Consultative Committee; the National Aboriginal Conference; the Aboriginal and Torres Straits Islander Commission; and the National Congress of Australia's First Peoples. Voter participation was low, rivalling achievements. The Aboriginal and Torres Straits Islander Commission (ATSIC) is perhaps the most obvious failure, collapsing under the weight of its own corruption and inertia in 2004. Tom Calma argues strongly that First Nations thrive when they have a say in their own lives. That may be more true than false, but the Voice could well prove to have little connection with Aboriginal life in the outback, and on the perimeters of country towns.

### 4. Its vagueness

The final report of the Indigenous Voice Co-design Process was released to the Australian government in July 2021. For all its 272 pages, it was less than specific as to what the Voice would entail. Linda Burney has made a virtue of its vagueness as she considers that the referendum on the Republic in 1999 was lost because it was too specific.

It is often maintained that only a 'modest' change is being suggested, but the Voice will have the right to comment on 'matters relating to Aboriginal and Torres Strait Islander peoples'. It could be easily argued that all matters affect the Aboriginal people, as they affect all Australians in general, so the Voice could speak on the Budget (as Robert Gottliebsen warns), foreign policy, education, infrastructure, and anything else on or near the agenda. The indigenous constitutional lawyer, Megan Davis, has admitted that 'virtually every issue' would be up for discussion. This should surprise no one, as there is no detail about the jurisdiction of the Voice, its powers, and its make-up. The law courts should get ready for plenty of business. Robert Gottliebsen speaks of decision-making being 'dramatically elongated', resulting in 'a High Court poker game'.[2] In fact, George Williams points out that the whole point of putting things in the Constitution is that it puts them beyond the parliament.[3]

Details as to how the Voice would work are, as Peter Kurti and Warren Mundine point out, 'vanishingly thin'.[4] Is it legislative or consultative? What if the Voice and the government of the day

---

2 Robert Gottliebsen, 'Voice will end federal budgets as we know them', in the *Australian*, 14 April 2023; 'Voice could dupe us all' in the *Australian,* 25 April 2023.

3 George Williams, 'Expect the courts to play a role in operation of voice' in the *Australian*, 21 May 2023; see also Janet Albrechtsen, 'Dear voters, please read this letter to appreciate what "Yes" will mean' in the *Weekend Australian,* 8-9 April 2023; and the *Australian,* 30 March 2023.

4 Peter Kurti and Warren Mundine (eds), 'Introduction' to *Beyond Belief,* Redland Bay: Connor Court Publishing, 2022, 2.

disagree? Louise Clegg has called it 'a fourth arm of government' – and she is a barrister.[5] The Voice could go to court on virtually anything. In theory it would not possess powers of veto, but in the present climate of political weakness and fear of the media, it would be likely to obstruct whatever it wanted to obstruct.

A treaty would actually mean 300 treaties, which is unworkable, and, in any case, surely implies compensation. Money has not solved indigenous problems in the past and is unlikely to in the future. The Treaty of Waitangi in New Zealand in 1840 had the advantage of being negotiated with one people group. Australian Aboriginal people consisted of about 300 different tribes with 300 different languages, spread out over a large continent and often at war with one another. There was no written language, and no concept of private property.

The Makarrata Commission has an Orwellian Ministry of Truth air about it. The likelihood of media show trials would be very high, and one set of distortions would replace another. Human truth is very mixed because we are all mixed – every person, of whatever nationality, is fallen, and prone to self-delusion. History is full of dreadful episodes – in 1838 at Myall Creek about 28 Aborigines, including women and children were massacred in cold blood, but seven men were hanged for the crime. In George Orwell's *Nineteen Eighty-Four,* history is distorted in order that the present might be controlled: 'Who controls the past controls the future; who controls the present controls the past'.[6] There may be real witches, but witch trials have a way of promoting fear and loathing.

5 Louise Clegg, 'Voice demands Constitutional Convention' in the *Australian,* 2 February 2023.

6 George Orwell, *Nineteen Eighty-Four,* part 3, chapter 2.

### 5. It makes the issue a constitutional one

Only 8 of 44 attempts at changing the Constitution have succeeded. Including Aborigines in the preamble of the Constitution failed in 1999, possibly because it was too full of windy rhetoric. The Voice could turn out to be an ATSIC which is enshrined in the Constitution and not easily dismantled. Section 51 of the Constitution gives the Parliament the capacity to create the Voice as a legislated body, which could be dismantled if it proved to be another failure.

An acknowledgment of Aboriginal settlement – or various settlements – in the preamble to the Constitution would seem to this non-lawyer to be far less problematic. It would be more symbolic than practical, but the Voice is likely to be both symbolic and impractical.

Henry Reynolds, a long-time student of Aboriginal history and its 'whispering in our hearts', warns that a failure for the 'Yes' in the referendum will mean that Australia's signing in 2009 of the UN Declaration on the Rights of Indigenous Peoples, will be used against us by UN activists.[7] What the world needs now is hardly more litigation.

### 6. There is no one Indigenous voice

There is an underlying assumption that the problems in Aboriginal societies are political when, in fact, they are more social and moral. Aboriginal societies in, say, Alice Springs, are unlikely be helped by another layer of elitist bureaucrats recycling their university essays in Aboriginal Studies. Black domestic violence is invariably greeted with a fearful silence, often for fear of being labelled 'racist'. European settlement in 1788 raised very serious difficulties for the Aboriginal people, but the issues now are

7 Henry Reynolds, 'If voice vote fails, expect radical call for global action' in the *Australian*, 3 May 2023.

different: welfare dependence, few economic opportunities in remote areas, the abuse of alcohol, the widespread use of drugs and pornography, the terrible scourge of domestic violence, and the communal ownership of land. There is a sad pattern, discerned by Peter Sutton, that the more government interference, the greater the deterioration.

Of the eleven Aboriginal members of federal parliament in 2023, who can claim to represent the indigenous voice? The aggressive, indeed strident, Lidia Thorpe? Or the vigorous but measured Jacinta Price? Noel Pearson has dismissed Jacinta Price as one who is caught in 'a tragic redneck celebrity vortex'. He labels Mrs Price and Warren Mundine as 'glove puppets' where 'the fists inside … punching down on Indigenous people are white.'[8] Good will is being lost.

Some Aboriginal people dislike the term 'Aboriginal'; some think 'indigenous' is inappropriate; some reject the language of 'First Nations' or 'tribes' and even prefer 'mobs'. Not all harm to Aborigines has been perpetrated by whites. In the Northern Territory there is far more likelihood of an Aborigine being hurt or killed by another Aborigine than by a white person. The belief that everything is explained by racism has done enormous harm in the real world. White families who have been foster carers of Aboriginal children for a decade or more have had bureaucrats remove those children without any consultation or explanation, or even visiting rights – a kind of stolen generation in reverse.

The numbers claiming to be Aboriginal or Torres Strait Islander has risen from about 116,000 in 1971 to over 800,000 in 2021. In many cases, no proof of identity is needed, just a claim, a ticking of the right box. If one's gender identity is a matter of choice, one supposes that the same could be true of one's ethnic identity.

8 Noel Pearson, 'The people will show the leadership our "leaders" lack' in the *Weekend Australian,* 20-21 May 2023.

### 7. At best this will probably be useless

The Voice is likely to become a preserve of the urban elites, with little connection to the real problems within aboriginal communities. Senator Jacinta Nampijinpa Price has consistently maintained that there is a self-serving Indigenous industry at work, and should the Voice succeed, Aboriginal people will forever be separate and perpetual victims.

Laws and finances will not usher in the millennium. The universal recognition given to Aboriginal peoples in 1967, a plethora of anti-discrimination laws, welfare to the tune of hundreds of millions of dollars – none of these measures have transformed Aboriginal life. There is nothing that quite rivals taxpayer-funded and bureaucratic-administered dysfunction.

Not all that promises goodness, delight and wisdom delivers – as Eve found out (Gen.3:6). The signs are not promising. In some quarters, including Aboriginal quarters, the prospect of the Voice has been met with indifference. In other quarters the language has been shrill, and often nasty. Noel Pearson has made helpful contributions in the past, especially in the field of Aboriginal education, but he has lost all proportion when it comes to the Voice. He accuses those who have doubts about it of being racists. Marcia Langton threatened that if the 'No' vote succeeded, there would be no more Welcomes to Country. Some might regard that as a double victory.

Sporting codes have fallen over themselves to promote a 'Yes' vote, as they did for same-sex marriage. The same can be said for business corporations, the universities, and the media in general. Even a NSW Supreme Court judge has accused a Nationals federal member of parliament of holding views that are 'disgusting', 'niggardly', 'cruel', 'mean-spirited' and 'racist' views because he and his party oppose the Voice. Those on the 'Yes' side have also been abused with foul language, as Chris Kenny has found out. Australians often pride themselves on a maturity they do not possess.

## 8. Conclusion

The Prime Minister, Anthony Albanese, has portrayed a 'Yes' vote as one of a line of incremental 'moments of truth' that include the Freedom Ride (a fifteen bus trip through regional NSW in 1965 to highlight the issue of racism, with key figures being Charles Perkins and Ted Noffs); the 1967 Referendum which included Aborigines in the Census; the Mabo decision of 1992 which recognised traditional lands as a form of permissive occupancy at the will of the Crown; the 1996 Wik decision which held that native title could co-exist on land held by pastoral leaseholders; the Redfern Speech of Prime Minister Paul Keating on 10 December 1992 which portrayed the oppressive side of European settlement in Australia; the Apology to the Stolen Generations issued by Prime Minister Kevin Rudd on 13 February 2008; and the photo of Gough Whitlam pouring red sand through the hands of the Aboriginal activist, Vincent Lingiari. Yet all this has coincided with a taxpayer-funded dysfunctionality in Aboriginal communities, especially in the outback, which unfortunately more than matches the dysfunctionality in other communities.

The Voice may prove to be a blessing or a risk to the fabric of Australian political life. Dr Johnson was once asked why he laughed at most schemes for political improvement, and he replied that 'most schemes of political improvement are very laughable things.'[9] The Voice is not likely to be laughable. Nothing fails quite like tokenism; hopes that are unrealised do more harm than daydreams. Aiming for reconciliation, it is likely to achieve

9 James Boswell, *The Life of Samuel Johnson*, London: Dent, reprinted 1973, vol 1, 374.

frustration and more grievance, irrespective of whether the Referendum succeeds or fails.

# 2

# THE VOICE AND THE PRINCIPLE OF 'POLITICAL EQUALITY'

**Gabriël A. Moens AM***

The government's present one-sided Voice narrative exposes advocates for the "No" campaign to claims of ignorance, even racism and bigotry.[1] Of course, such claims intimidate open-minded commentators, who are willing to debate the proposal to entrench the Voice in the Australian Constitution. Nevertheless, this book and its contributions provide its Australian readership with an alternative point of view to enable electors to make an informed decision on referendum day.

This chapter focuses on the Voice's extinguishment of the principle of 'political equality'. It also offers an assessment of the relationship between the Voice and section 116 of the Constitution – which deals with religious freedom. It is, however, useful to commence with a brief foray into the origins of the Voice and the initial political responses to the proposal.

---

* Gabriël Moens AM is Emeritus Professor of Law, The University of Queensland and co-author of Augusto Zimmermann & Gabriël Moens, *Foundations of the Australian Legal System: History, Theory and Practice*, LexisNexis, 2023.

1 See Nyunggeri Warren Mundine, 'Don't paint indigenous opponents of the Voice as race-baiters', *The Centre for Independent Studies*, 9 December 2022, at https://www.cis.org.au/commentary/opinion/dont-paint-indigenous-opponents-of-the-voice-as-race-baiters/.

## 1. The origins of the Voice and initial responses

In July 2020, the former Coalition government, and the Coalition of Peaks – the Coalition of Aboriginal and Torres Strait Islander Peak Organisations – proposed the National Agreement on Closing the Gap. This Agreement "stems from the belief that when Aboriginal and Torres Strait Islander people have a genuine say in the design and delivery of services that affect them, better life outcomes are achieved." However, the former Prime Minister, Scott Morrison indicated that his government did not propose to enshrine the Voice into the Constitution. Instead, he favoured the legislative establishment of such a body, to be called 'Voice to government'.

Of course, Australia's Aboriginal people are already well represented in parliament by eleven Indigenous parliamentarians. Considering that Australia's Indigenous population is estimated to constitute 3.2 percent of the total population, this group is over-represented in parliament. It is also the only racial group that has its own federal minister, and every state and territory has a Ministry for Indigenous Affairs.

The Voice is the current Labor government's response to the recommendations made by an Aboriginal National Constitutional Convention held in 2017 near Uluru, which resulted in the release of a document, the *Uluru Statement from the Heart*. There is no denying the reality that this Statement galvanised a movement to amend the Australian Constitution. It invites people to walk with Aboriginals and Torres Strait Islander people "in a movement of the Australian people for a better future."[2]

The Statement proposes the establishment of an Indigenous

2 The Uluru Statement from the Heart is available at: https://ulurustatemdev.wpengine.com/wp-content/uploads/2022/01/UluruStatementfromtheHeartPLAINTEXT.pdf.

Voice to parliament, and the Makarrata Commission to supervise a process of agreement-making with Australian governments and oversee a process of truth-telling about Australia's history and colonisation.

On 30 July 2022, Prime Minister Anthony Albanese used an address at the Garma Indigenous Festival in the Northern Territory to declare his unqualified support for the Voice and to reveal the referendum question which may be put to the Australian people. The question is: "Do you support an alteration to the Constitution that establishes an Aboriginal and Torres Strait Islander Voice?"

The Prime Minister also indicated that three provisions be added to the Constitution if the referendum were to succeed.

> *Chapter IX*
>
> *Recognition of Aboriginal and Torres Strait Islander Peoples*
>
> *129 Aboriginal and Torres Strait Islander Voice*
>
> *In recognition of Aboriginal and Torres Strait Islander peoples as the First Peoples of Australia: (i) there shall be a body, to be called the Aboriginal and Torres Strait Islander Voice; (ii) the Aboriginal and Torres Strait Islander Voice may make representations to the Parliament and the Executive Government of the Commonwealth on matters relating to Aboriginal and Torres Strait Islander peoples; (iii) the Parliament shall, subject to this Constitution, have power to make laws with respect to matters relating to the Aboriginal and Torres Strait Islander Voice, including its composition, functions, powers and procedures.*

Thus, the proposal provides for the "Voice" to have its own chapter (Chapter IX) in the Constitution, alongside the Legislature, the Executive Government, and the Judicature. The first provision would entrench the Voice in the Constitution;

the second would allow the Voice to make 'representations' to parliament and the executive government on matters relating to Indigenous Australians. The third proposes to insert, into the Constitution, a new head of legislative power, according to which the parliament shall have power to make laws with respect to the functions and procedures of the Voice.

The Leader of the Nationals Party, David Littleproud, announced on 28 November 2022 that his Party does not support the Voice. The party's representatives argue that all people, regardless of race, who are dispossessed, or are disadvantaged, should be assisted. Similarly, the Liberal Party decided in April 2023 to campaign for a 'No' vote. Consequently, Julian Leeser, who served as Shadow Minister for Indigenous Affairs at the time, relinquished his position because he favours the Voice. The Opposition Leader, Peter Dutton, then appointed the indomitable Senator Jacinta Price to become the Shadow Minister. Also, prominent commentator Warren Mundine, a former National President of the Labor Party, and Gary Johns, a former Labor Minister in the Keating government, are members of the Advance's Fair Australia 'No' campaign.

Over the years, there have been countless, and sometimes corrupt, Aboriginal quangos, like the Australian and Torres Straits Islander Commission ("ATSIC"), that have wasted millions of dollars. By any standard, the Indigenous industry has spawned the creation of huge, bloated bureaucracies, the maintenance of which is expensive. Often, these administrative behemoths have designed and administered doomed policies, including the cashless credit card, alcohol prohibition, housing, and social welfare programmes.

If these precedents are an indication, there is no hope that the Voice would be any better. In fact, it would be far worse because it would be impossible to remove a body that is entrenched in the Constitution since it could only be terminated in accordance with section 128 of the Constitution, which requires a referendum and a double majority – a majority of electors, and a majority of States.

### 2. The violation of the principle of 'political equality' and 'equal citizenship'

The most important flaw in the potential enshrinement of the Voice in the Constitution is its granting of special privileges to one group merely on the ground of the race of its members. The distribution of societal benefits and burdens on the ground of a person's race, which is an involuntary characteristic over which people have no control – an incident of birth – makes a mockery of governments' stated reassurances to create a society where a person's race is irrelevant, and the administration of justice is colour-blind.

The proposed addition to the Constitution envisages that the Voice would be a standing advisory body, consisting of twenty-four members, that may make 'representations' to the parliament and the executive on laws and policies affecting Indigenous people in Australia. Although the word 'representation' does not require the legislature and the executive to consult, and seek the advice of, the 'Voice', it is expected that the Voice will need to be consulted when the governing party, which would have a majority in the House of Representatives, proposes to adopt laws.[3] If so, the requirement of 'consultation' raises the question of whether it would be sufficient to ask the Voice for advice, or whether it must actually give advice. If the latter,

3 See John Andrianao, 'The meaning of treaty, rejection of unity, and a two-state system', *The Spectator*, 6 June 2023, at https://www.spectator.com.au/2023/06/the-meaning-of-treaty-rejection-of-unity-and-a-two-state-system/.

and the adoption of legislation were delayed until the Voice provides its advice, it could effectively stymie the governance of the country by adopting the convenient device of not giving an opinion at all, thereby arrogating to itself a veto power, and paralysing the machinery of government. In such a case, the Voice would effectively function as a third chamber in addition to the House of Representatives and the Senate.

Of course, implementing legislation could seek to restrict the advisory power of the Voice to a consideration of proposed laws and policies that actually or potentially affect Indigenous people. However, such an approach is impractical because all general laws, since they are (or should be) made for all the people of Australia, potentially impact on Indigenous Australians. Indeed, unless the government wants to create an institutionalised form of apartheid, it is not appropriate to exempt any racial group from the application of Australia's general laws.

In addition, the determination of "the composition, functions, powers and procedures" of the Voice would require the parliament to draft detailed rules on establishing group membership. This would lead to intractable problems associated with attempts to prove membership of a group – a type of purity law, reminiscent of the racial laws of Nazi Germany. Alternatively, if membership were to be determined by self-identification, then this would in all likelihood result in an over-inclusive extension of the concept of 'Indigenous' Australians. The sponsors of the Voice may attempt to sidestep this difficulty by arguing that 'societal disadvantage', which is much easier to determine, is a suitable proxy for determining group membership. Such an attempt has merit, but it still raises the question of why one disadvantaged group, among others, is selected for special treatment.

In reality, there is utter confusion as to who is to be regarded as 'Indigenous', how the twenty-four members of the Voice will be chosen, and what the powers of that 'advisory' body' will be. Indeed, in Australia, 'Aboriginality' seems to have developed into an amorphous, undefinable concept that has steadily been expanded to cover cultural traits that are different from the mainstream population. If membership of the Voice were to be determined, not on the basis of strict guidelines that define 'Aboriginality', the proposed body could be used to drive a wedge between people, not bringing them together, as the Uluru Statement from the Heart wants us to believe.

Hence, the Voice may result in the allocation of group rights and separate rights for a racial group. This may well constitute a violation of the United Nations International Convention on the Elimination of All Forms of Racial Discrimination. The Convention stipulates in Article 1(4) that: "Special measures taken for the sole purpose of securing adequate advancement of certain racial or ethnic groups ... shall not be deemed racial discrimination, provided, however, that that such measures do not, as a consequence, lead to the maintenance of separate rights for different racial groups and that they shall not be continued after the objectives for which they were taken have been achieved." The enshrinement of the Voice in the Constitution would clearly offend this Convention, thus institutionalising discrimination in Australia and potentially affecting all aspects of society.

## 3. The Voice and 'reconciliation'

The Voice is often promoted as the ideal vehicle to achieve 'reconciliation' between Indigenous and non-Indigenous Australians. The media is effectively treating the Voice as a byword for 'reconciliation', which has become one of the most used but least understood words in political and social discourse. Often, it simply means the adoption of a swath of privileges available only to those who identify as Indigenous.

Commenting on the present 'reconciliation' developments, Peter O'Brien states that, "so far, non-indigenous Australia has done all the reconciling—witness the ubiquity of the Aboriginal flag, the constant refrains of 'we acknowledge the traditional owners,' the Aboriginal domination of the opening ceremonies of all major public events, the Aboriginal-only study grants and job placements, the relinquishment of 60 percent of our land mass to some form of native title, and so on almost *ad infinitum*."[4]

In contrast, proponents of the Voice argue that the 'invasion' and consequent disruption of the cultures of Aboriginal tribes in Australia necessitates 'reconciliation' as an atonement for taking the land of the inhabitants who were there at the time of European settlement. However, why should this now result in a huge race-based industry to reconcile with those who claim special privileges because of their race?

Throughout recorded history, powerful countries have invaded weaker countries and acquired them by force or settlement. Mostly, these unfortunate events have not resulted in demands for reparation, compensation, or reconciliation. Why, then, would it be different in Australia? Indeed, in Australia, the accommodating attitude displayed by various Australian governments to the interests of Indigenous Australians borders on abdication of responsibility, portraying Indigenous Australians as 'victims' and imbuing non-Indigenous Australians with a guilt complex. As pointed out by O'Brien, this view is lent credence by the abundance and ubiquity of

4 Peter O'Brien, 'The Magic Pudding of 'Reconciliation'', *Quadrant Online*, 5 December 2022, at https://quadrant.org.au/opinion/aborigines/2022/12/the-magic-pudding-of-reconciliation/. See also James Jeffery, 'Five Reasons Christians Should Reject the Voice', *Quadrant Online*, 25 June 2023, at. https://quadrant.org.au/opinion/religion/2023/06/five-reasons-christians-should-reject-the-voice/.

'Welcome to Country' ceremonies and 'cultural' performances, which have become permanent, if not compulsory, accessories to all academic, social, corporate, and sporting events.

Australia is unique in that it seeks to undo the past by enthusiastically promoting the Voice as a way of achieving reconciliation. This movement seeks to atone for the 'invasion' of Australia by Captain Arthur Phillip on 26 January 1788, following Lieutenant James Cook's decision to claim the East Coast of Australia for the British on 22 August 1770.

On 26 January 2023, against a background of left-wing demonstrators protesting for constitutional recognition at 'Invasion Day' rallies, the Prime Minster, Anthony Albanese, told a media conference in Tasmania:

> *Across the country, every state premier, every chief minister, is supporting Yes at this referendum because this is about progress going forward. It is about reconciliation. It's not a radical proposition. So I'm not surprised that some radicals are opposed to it. Because this is a mainstream proposition. This is a modest and gracious request for reconciliation by Aboriginal and Torres Strait Islander peoples.*[5]

By contrast, Keith Windschuttle argues that "the proposed Voice or its variants would all be the opposite of reconciliation. The goal has always been political power and who will have ultimate sovereignty on this continent."[6]

---

5 Reported by Maeve Bannister, 'PM dismisses 'radical' opposition to voice', *The Canberra Times*, 27 January 2023, at https://www.canberratimes.com.au/story/8062939/pm-dismisses-radical-opposition-to-voice/.

6 Keith Windschuttle, 'Living on Stolen Land', *Quadrant Online*, 27 February 2023, at https://quadrant.org.au/magazine/2023/03/living-on-stolen-land/.

## 4. The new discrimination

When the successful 1967 referendum, which empowered the Federal Parliament to make laws for "The people of any race for whom it is deemed necessary to make special laws" was held, there was a general expectation that Australia would finally become a colour-blind society. In a colour-blind society, the distribution of societal burdens and benefits would not depend on a person's race – an involuntary characteristic over which people have no control. The Parliament thus has the power to adopt legislation which removes impediments to ensure that members of any race become full members of the polity. The new powers of the Parliament were expected to cement the principle of 'political equality' and 'equal citizenship' in the political DNA of Australia. As such, it is a worthy principle, implementation of which enhances the equal treatment of all members of society and confirms that, from a political point of view, they are deemed to be of equal standing. For example, a manifestation of the principle of 'political equality' is that all electors have one equal vote and do not benefit from favoured or preferential treatment.

In contrast, the Voice is about exploiting differences between racial groups, only giving a voice to people deemed to be part of the favoured elites. Indeed, the gains of 1967 would be undone if the Voice referendum were to be successful because it would enshrine discrimination forever into the Constitution, and Australia would be a racist country where burdens and benefits are distributed based on characteristics that have nothing to do with merit, but everything to do with political expediency.

In reality, the promise of 'political equality' has been progressively emasculated since the adoption of the *Racial Discrimination Act* 1975, which facilitated the implementation of various forms of affirmative action, coupled with growing advocacy by Australia's

Indigenous activists. These developments confirmed that a colour-blind society is merely a lofty aspiration, easily punctured or extinguished by the ruling illiberal elites, who advocate for a more radical form of equality of results or outcome.

Yet, proponents of the Voice speciously argue that it is a 'modest' proposal. However, experience indicates that when government officials talk about 'modest' reform, they are usually trying to hide the monumental and disruptive impact which the proposal, if successful, will have on society. Indeed, it could be expected that a failure by the legislator or executive to seek the advice of the Voice may well be challenged in the High Court. Hence, we might see increased judicial activity and adventurism, which would enmesh the judiciary in conflicts which are of a political nature. Specifically, members of the Voice may seek out activist judges claiming that this body should have been consulted, thereby causing delay and confusion. Hence, "What is being promoted as healing and reconciling is in practice dividing and alienating."[7]

## 5. The Voice constitutes a violation of section 116 of the Constitution.

The Uluru Statement from the Heart, after stating that the Indigenous tribes "were the first sovereign Nations of the Australian continent", confidently declares:

> *This sovereignty is a spiritual notion: the ancestral tie between the land, or 'mother nature', and the Aboriginal and Torres Strait Islander peoples who were born therefrom, remain attached thereto, and must one day return thither to be united with our ancestors. This link is the basis of the ownership of the soil, or better, of sovereignty.*

7 Eric Abetz, 'The Multiple Fallacies Contained Within the Voice to Parliament', *The Epoch Times*, 2 February 2023, at https://www.theepochtimes.com/the-multiple-fallacies-contained-within-the-voice-to-parliament_5030708.html.

Dave Pellowe, referring to this Statement in an episode of *The Church and State Show*, remarked that "It is a religious text, laden with pagan beliefs like animism and ancestor worship. It literally describes Aboriginal sovereignty over this continent as a spiritual and sacred notion: the land as an entity they are born from, remain attached to and return to upon their death. The text's supporters agree this religious belief is the basis of Aboriginal ownership of the land." He concludes that, if his assessment of the Statement is correct, then it comes "awfully close to violating Section 116 of the Constitution." Pellowe's view offers an interesting perspective, and it merits further elaboration.

Section 116 of the Constitution stipulates that "The Commonwealth shall not make any law for establishing any religion, or for imposing any religious observance … and no religious test shall be required as a qualification for any office or public trust under the Commonwealth."

Any assessment of the Uluru Statement from the Heart in the light of Section 116 of the Constitution must obviously seek to ascertain whether the Statement constitutes a 'religion', consisting of beliefs, ideas, and practices which are religious in character and are relied upon by the Government in its push to entrench the Voice in the Constitution.

The High Court has indicated that it is difficult, even daunting, to attempt to define the concept of 'religion'. This difficulty was acknowledged by Latham C.J. in *Adelaide Company of Jehovah's Witnesses Inc v Commonwealth*, when he said that "It would be difficult, if not impossible, to devise a definition of religion which would satisfy the adherents of all the many and various religions which exist or have existed."[8]

8 (1943) 67 CLR 116, 123.

Indeed, it is not surprising for the High Court, when faced with the issue of determining whether a particular set of beliefs constitutes 'religion', to highlight the difficulties which are invariably associated with any attempt to define the term. For example, in *Church of the New Faith v. Commissioner for Pay -Roll Tax (Vic.),* the High Court was asked to determine whether the tenets of the Church of Scientology constitute religion for the purposes of section 116 of the Constitution. An affirmative answer would have made the church eligible to apply for tax-exempt status. Although "an excess of verbiage" was devoted to the extrapolation of the tests or criteria of a religion, confusion remained. Mason C.J. and Brennan J. argued that "for the purposes of the law, the criteria of religion are twofold; first, belief in a supernatural Being, Thing or Principle; and second, the acceptance of canons of conduct in order to give effect to that belief."[9] This opinion is interesting because it suggests that belief which does not require action in accordance with these beliefs might not be sufficient to constitute a religion. Similarly, Wilson J. and Deane J. submitted that a set of beliefs which do not relate to things supernatural, is not likely to be recognised as a religion.[10]

If the High Court were to liberally interpret the concept of 'religion' as embracing any set of ideas and practices, which one believes will lead to liberation or fulfilment of one's being, then the Uluru Statement from the Heart would certainly qualify as 'religion'. The description, in the Statement, of 'sovereignty' as a "spiritual notion" that encapsulates the belief of Indigenous people surely comes close to a "Supernatural ... Thing or Principle" which serves as the rallying point of those who want to entrench the Voice in the Constitution. Of course, a liberal and wide definition of 'religion', which involves the characterisation of any set of beliefs as religion, would be open to the objection that it is operationally meaningless since it is incapable of being used to recognise various kinds of beliefs.

9 (1983) 154 CLR 120, 134-135.

10 Ibid, at 147.

In this context, it could be asked whether governments (and even courts) have a right to examine whether a set of beliefs constitutes a 'religion'. This is because a set of beliefs may be regarded by its adherents as constituting a religion, even though they may not come within the criteria applied by the High Court or the ruling elites. But, in the case of the *Uluru Statement from the Heart*, the religious foundations of the Voice based on 'sovereignty' as a 'spiritual notion' can hardly be denied.

The religious nature of the *Uluru Statement from the Heart* is relevant because the Voice proposal is based on, and inspired by, this Statement. The Government's unqualified adoption and implementation of the Statement and its tenacious promotion of the Voice could thus be characterised as an establishment of religion in Australia and the imposition of religious observance on people in society. This is certainly happening in Australia where the Indigenous industry is bureaucratised, and the alleged advantages of the Voice are promoted as gospel-like truths. In addition, those who aspire to serve on the Voice, if it were to be successful, would need to qualify as ardent proponents of the Statement, thereby also potentially violating the Constitutional directive that no religious test shall be used to determine the suitability of people for government positions. The Voice may thus well violate section 116 of the Constitution.

## 6. Concluding comments

The Voice represents the triumph of symbolism over substance. These days, politicians are prepared to spend millions of dollars on symbolism, but ultimately meaningless gestures, like permanently raising the Aboriginal flag over the Sydney Harbour Bridge. We live in an era where symbolism is regarded as social 'progress' even if it results in the unequal treatment of Australians, involving the creation of a race-based society.

Is it believable that the Voice will make a measurable difference for Indigenous Australians? Will it curb the riots and crime spree in Alice Springs? Reduce addictions? Eliminate child abuse? Decrease alcohol dependency? Will it increase the lifespan of Indigenous Australians? Better health outcomes? In this context, it is reasonable to consider whether it would not be better to make direct aid available to encourage Indigenous Australians to look after themselves by reducing, or even eliminating, their dependence on an all-powerful state.

In this context, Eric Abetz offered his view that "Not one life will be improved by the proposed change. But if the funds wasted in pursuit of the Voice were spent on law enforcement and school attendance a rapid increase in the wellbeing of our Indigenous communities would be there for all to witness." He says that "To treat or prioritise one group over another is discriminatory and inequitable."[11]

If the Voice proposal is successful, will that be the end of Indigenous claims? Such an outcome is unlikely. There are those who want to burn Australia to the ground, and do not want to give advice to a 'colonial' government. Keith Windschuttle convincingly explains that the Voice is about 'sovereignty', carving out a separate state which would necessitate Australia to enter into international treaties with First Nations people under applicable international law rules.

If electors want to ascertain how the Voice might work, they should consider the experiences of other countries where similar developments have taken place. For example, in New Zealand, which has an advisory Maori body, there are five dedicated seats in parliament for the Maoris. So, it is legitimate to ask the question whether, eventually, the Voice project might lead to separate and dedicated seats for Indigenous people in parliament.

11 See. n. 7.

Henry Ergas, in an article entitled *The Voice in the Light of the Western Intellectual Tradition* argues that Australians are led to believe "that constitutionalising inequality will promote equality and that enshrining separateness will reinforce national unity."[12] However, the reality is that, in enshrining the Voice in the Constitution, Australia will become a racist country, divided along racial lines, where burdens and benefits are distributed on the ground of race.

Surely, such a development belittles the often-stated claim that a person's rights, obligations, and privileges should not be dependent on a characteristic over which people have no control and therefore is irrelevant in the distribution of burdens of benefits.

The only viable approach is to vote 'No' on referendum day.

12 Henry Ergas, ' The Voice in the Light of the Western Intellectual Tradition', *Beyond Belief: Rethinking the Voice to Parliament* (eds Peter Kurti & Warren Mundine AO), Connor Court Publishing, 2022, 169.

# 3

# THE HIDDEN AGENDA BEHIND A "VOICE" TO PARLIAMENT

**Augusto Zimmermann***

Australia's Prime Minister, Anthony Albanese, with the support of all the state and territory premiers, has officially backed the "First Nations Voice" – a standing consultative body to advise the government on laws and policies arguably affecting the Aboriginal community but, potentially, the nation as a whole. He says it is a priority for the government to secure a successful referendum that will constitutionally entrench this "consultative body".[1]

In past referenda, Australian governments at least pretended to foster fair debate by providing electors with pamphlets listing the official arguments for and against the proposed changes. At this time, however, says Senator Pat Dodson, the prime minister's special envoy for the implementation of the Voice, "the government is not interested to support any racist campaigns, which will have

---

* Augusto Zimmermann is Head and Professor of Law at Sheridan Institute of Higher Education and co-author of Augusto Zimmermann & Gabriël Moens, *Foundations of the Australian Legal System: History, Theory and Practice*, LexisNexis, 2023. He is also President of the Western Australian Legal Theory Association (WALTA) and a former law reform commissioner with the Law Reform Commission of Western Australia.

1 Lorena Allam and Sarah Collard, 'PM, state and territory leaders formally back Indigenous voice to parliament with statement of intent', *The Guardian*, 3 February 2023, at https://www.theguardian.com/australia-news/2023/feb/03/pm-state-and-territory-leaders-formally-back-indigenous-voice-to-parliament-with-statement-of-intent

an impact on the question of the pamphlet".[2]

This seems to confirm what Anthony Dillon, an Australian Aborigine academic, thinks about the present discussion of Aboriginal issues. "There seems to be no end to where offence can be taken and accusations of racism made", he says.[3] Hence, it may be necessary for me to disclose that I am a strong supporter of the right of Australian Aborigines to freely embrace, practise and celebrate their cultural heritage without governmental interference.

## 1. Undermining Political Equality

Proponents of an "Indigenous Voice" to Parliament often condone a violation of the principle of equality before the law so as to atone for all the possible violations of equality in the past. And yet, they fail to explain how it is possible to correct past discrimination by ultimately condoning the entrenchment in the Constitution of a divisive system that will violate the equal treatment of all citizens in the future.

The Australian Constitution is primarily based on the principle of equality of all citizens before the law. Accordingly, one of the great virtues of our Constitution is its equal treatment of all citizens. This is the nation's fundamental law for all Australians regardless of origin, culture, or ethnicity. It is, therefore. improper to use this basic law to promote one group over the rest of the population.

However, Australians will soon be asked to introduce into their Constitution the undemocratic element of racial preference.

2 Chris Merritt, 'The Voice: The Case for Voting No', The Rule of Law Education Centre, at https://www.ruleoflaw.org.au/voice-the-case-for-voting-no/

3 Anthony Dillon, 'Recognising May Mean Never Closing the Gap', *in* Gary Johns (ed.) *Recognise What? Arguments to Acknowledge Aboriginal Culture or rights, in the Australian Constitution* (Connor Court Publishing, 2014) 55.

According to Chris Merritt, vice-president of *The Rule of Law Institute of Australia,* this will be about asking the Australian people to give one racial group – and their descendants for all time – constitutionally guaranteed additional influence over all areas of public office.[4]

In their eagerness to promote the idea, advocates for the Voice to parliament often embrace the view that Indigenous Australians were "excluded from the Constitution of 1901 under a clause that said they should not be counted."[5] Apparently, these advocates rely on Section 25 of the Constitution to allege such "exclusion", which is often provided as proof that this fundamental document contemplates a denial of the franchise on racial grounds. This Section reads:

> *...if by the law of any State all persons of any race are disqualified from voting at elections for the more numerous House of the Parliament of the State, then, in reckoning the number of the people of the State or of the Commonwealth, persons of that race resident in that State shall not be counted.*

In reality, this provision was included in the Constitution because, in the 1890s, Queensland and Western Australia still practised racial discrimination by not allowing people of exclusive Aboriginal ethnicity to vote in state elections.[6] The framers opposed this heinous practice and wanted to bring those states into line with all the others, where Aborigines already had the franchise. Accordingly, Section 25 is actually an *anti-racist* provision designed to penalise those Australian states, that still discriminated against

4 Merritt, n. 2.

5 Shireen Morris, 'Yes Is for Bringing Australia Together and Moving Forward', *The Epoch Times*, May 2, 2023, at https://www.theepochtimes.com/yes-is-for-bringing-australia-together-and-moving-forward_5235224.html.

6 Gabriël A. Moens AM and Augusto Zimmermann, 'Does the Uluru Statement from the Heart violate the Constitution?, *The Spectator Australia*, 24 April 2023, at https://www.spectator.com.au/2023/04/does-the-uluru-statement-from-the-heart-violate-the-constitution/.

Aborigines, by reducing their representation in the newly created Commonwealth Parliament.

There is also the problem of advancing undemocratic representation. For one thing, details about what the Voice as a "consultative body" would look like, and how it would function, is one of the matters which are left unaddressed – perhaps intentionally so. Instead, the final report of the *Indigenous Voice Co-Design Process* raises the prospect that at least some Voice members would not be directly chosen by the Indigenous community but nominated by the local and regional "Voices."

"Sadly, this is the enduring legacy of Aboriginal affairs in Australia," says Dallas Scott, an Aboriginal blogger who is very proud of his cultural heritage. He talks about the dominance within the Indigenous communities of self-appointed "leaders" who often make important decisions for others and speak for them. According to Scott, titles such as "Aboriginal elder", "spokesperson" and "tribal leader" (or some other colourful variations) are often given to individuals who are not elected by those who they claim to represent, but overwhelmingly, who are self-appointed to such leadership roles.[7]

In a society where people have been sent to die for the chance to bring democracy to another country, turning a blind eye to the undemocratic nature of native organisations is quite appalling, indeed.

## 2. Aggravating Dependence on Government

Supporters of "Indigenous Voice" often claim that this will improve practical outcomes in Indigenous communities. This is

7 Dallas Scott, 'Fighting a War Already Won', in: Gary Johns (ed.) *Recognise What? Arguments to Acknowledge Aboriginal Culture or Rights in the Australian Constitution* (Connor Court, 2014) 80.

an assertion, nothing more. Of course, it is not unusual for laws and policies, although well-intentioned, to have the opposite effect as that allegedly contemplated. Arguably, modern Australia's worst Indigenous suffering and deprivation in the dysfunctional remote 'homeland' communities have been greatly caused by the continuing implementation by Australian governments of the welfare policies which began in the 1970s.[8]

Since the Second World War, governments around Australia have maintained and nurtured a burgeoning and expensive bureaucracy focused on the welfare of the Aboriginal community. And yet, welfare dependence has actually *aggravated* the conditions which have perpetuated poverty and dependence in the Aboriginal community. Decades of federal, state and territory policies have miserably failed to improve the lives of Australia's most disadvantaged peoples. Currently, more than half (53%) of all the Indigenous Australians aged 16 and over are receiving some form of Centrelink income support payment, compared with 26% of non-Indigenous Australians of this age.[9]

To a great extent, any behaviour that government rewards generally tends to increase. As such, the prevalence of passive welfare dependence in the Indigenous communities appears to be directly responsible for the scourge of drugs, pornography, child abuse, and the effects of 'humbugging'.[10] The point is that government programs to help welfare recipients tend to exacerbate these problems. By handing out welfare checks impersonally to

8 Bernard Samuelson, 'What Conservative Voice Supporters Get Wrong About Constitutional Recognition', in Peter Kurti and Warren Mundine AO, *Beyond Belief: Rethinking the Voice to Parliament* (Connor Court Publishing, 2022) 61.

9 At https://www.aihw.gov.au/reports/australias-welfare/indigenous-income-and-finance See also: https://www.aihw.gov.au/getmedia/2f327206-c315-43a7-b666-4fe24fefc12f/aihw-australias-welfare-2017-chapter7-5.pdf.

10 Gary Johns, 'Introduction', *in* Gary Johns (ed.) *Recognise What? Arguments to Acknowledge Aboriginal Culture or Rights in the Australian Constitution* (Connor Court Publishing, 2014) 15.

all who potentially qualify, without addressing the underlying behavioural problems, the government in essence 'rewards' dysfunctional behaviour that affects not only the recipient but their community at large.

Perhaps nobody has better expressed the "evil results of a too excessive solicitude on the part of the State", than the classical liberal philosopher of the 19th century, Wilhelm von Humboldt (1767 – 1835). This German philosopher, linguist, diplomat, and founder of the Humboldt University of Berlin, was described by Friedrich Hayek as "Germany's greatest philosopher of freedom." In Chapter III of *The Limits of State Action,* Humboldt teaches us this important lesson, one that should be learned by every Australian, Aboriginal or not:

> *The evil results of a too extensive solicitude on the part of the State, are still more strikingly shown in the suppression of all active energy, and the necessary deterioration of the moral character. ... The idea of the first no longer inspire him; and the painful consciousness of the last assails him less frequently and forcibly, since he can more easily ascribe his shortcomings to this particular position, and leave them to the responsibility of those who have made it what it is.*
>
> *If we add to this, that he may not, possibly, regard the designs of the State as perfectly pure in their objects or execution – that he may suspect that his own advantage only, but along with it some other additional purpose is intended, then, not only the force and energy, but also the purity of his moral nature suffers. He now conceives himself not only completely free from any duty which the State has not expressly imposed upon him, but exonerated at the same time from every personal effort to improve his own condition; and, even fears such an effort, as if it were likely to open out new opportunities, of which the State might take advantage...*

> *Further, the pernicious influence of such a positive policy is no less evident in the behaviour of the citizens to each other. As each individual abandons himself to the solicitous aid of the State, so, and still more, he abandons to it the fate of his fellow-citizens. This weakens sympathy and renders mutual assistance inactive: … and experience teaches us that oppressed classes of the community which are, as it were, overlooked by the government, are always bound together by the closest ties. But whether the citizen becomes indifferent to his fellows, so will the husband be to his wife, and the father of a family towards the members of this household.*[11]

Advocates for the Voice often talk about self-determination and empowerment. They fail to demonstrate how these objectives can be achieved without the Aborigines taking full responsibility for themselves, their family, and their community at large. Of course, self-determination would require Aborigines to make their own decisions and support themselves and their families without any form of governmental dependency and bureaucratic oversight. According to Nyunggai Warren Mundine AO, an Aboriginal businessman who was the national president of the Australian Labor Party,

> *There can be no self-determination or autonomy for any community if there is total dependence on governments and bureaucracies, or if there is no real economy. No country or community can survive without an economy to support it. The greatest threat to Indigenous Australians living on country remove and regional Australia is chronic dependence on government without needing meaningfully to contribute in return.*[12]

11 Wilhelm von Humboldt, *The Limits of State Action*, Chapter III.

12 Nyunggai Warren Mundine AO, 'The Indigenous Voice Does Not Speak For Country', in Peter Kurti and Warren Mundine AO, *Beyond Belief: Rethinking the Voice to Parliament* (Connor Court Publishing, 2022) 85.

The Australian government is now dedicated to upholding the Uluru Statement from the Heart as a constitutionally enshrined "Voice" to Parliament. What is particularly problematic about such statement is that it shifts accountability and accomplishments from the individuals involved to the culturally defined group. As noted by Amanda Stoker, a former Liberal Senator, this appeal to the group represents a shift away from personal responsibility to the more collectivist notion that "individuals are valued based on genetic attributes over which they have no control, rather than on the content of their character".[13] The problem, she says, is that "when group identity is the organising principle, individuals don't bear any responsibility for their part in the decisions that have led to their lives outcomes".[14]

The Voice, in its practical operation, will enshrine in the Constitution a socially harmful separatist approach to Indigenous affairs. Any reluctance to listen to the Voice will be sure to trigger accusations of a return to pre-Voice days.[15] By functioning as the mouthpiece of the Aboriginal industry, "the Voice will have a powerful and permanent position from which both to shape the political narrative around Indigenous affairs and to persuade parliament not to adopt policies deemed to be against Indigenous interests because the measures were considered unfair and discriminatory".[16] Of course, for the reasons stated above, further empowering a self-serving "industry" that seeks to maintain its own relevance will not help to advance the well-being of Australia's Indigenous peoples, and quite to the contrary.

---

13 Amanda Stoker, 'Head Over Heart: The Legal, Democratic and Practical Problems Raised by the Uluru Statement', in Peter Kurti and Warren Mundine AO, *Beyond Belief: Rethinking the Voice to Parliament* (Connor Court Publishing, 2022) 90.

14 Stoker, n. 13, 91.

15 Samuelson, n. 8, 68.

16 Ibid.

### 3. The Advocacy of Inequality

The ruling classes are presently pushing the argument that the constitutional entrenchment of an "Indigenous Voice" will be just about providing advice to government on matters affecting the Aboriginal communities.[17] However, every single law in this country should affect Aboriginal people because they are part of the larger Australian community. Although the Voice, apparently, would only be consulted if proposed laws and policies directly affect Aboriginal people, such argument is fallacious because all laws are (and should be) made for all the people of Australia. In other words, "matters" relating to Aboriginal and Torres Strait Islander peoples actually means everything. As Mundine correctly points out,

> *Indigenous Australians are Australians citizens. There is no law, regulation or policy, nor any act or decision of the Federal government or parliament, that doesn't relate to Aboriginal and Torres Strait Islander people. Energy. Mining. Tax. Defence. Natural security. Trade and commerce. Health. Education. Foreign Affairs. All are 'matters' relating to Aboriginal and Torres Strait Islander peoples.*[18]

Arguably, "a Voice to Parliament will give Indigenous communities a route to help inform policy and legal decisions that impact their lives".[19] This presupposes an inherent difference between Aboriginal Australians and non-Aboriginal Australians, which may send an unconsciously *racist* message that Australian Aborigines can never be fully integrated as active members of

17 Anthony Dillon, 'The Voice: Self-Determination or Separatism?', in Peter Kurti and Warren Mundine AO, *Beyond Belief: Rethinking the Voice to Parliament* (Connor Court Publishing, 2022) 15.

18 Nyunggai Warren Mundine, 'The Indigenous Voice Does Not Speak for the Country', in Peter Kurti and Warren Mundine AO, *Beyond Belief: Rethinking the Voice to Parliament* (Connor Court Publishing, 2022) 78.

19 'Voice to Parliament', *Reconciliation Australia*, at https://www.reconciliation.org.au/reconciliation/support-a-voice-to-parliament/.

the broader community. After all, why not expect that in the not so distant future a person of Aboriginal heritage could actually become the Prime Minister of Australia? As Kurti and Mundine properly remind us,

> *The 2022 federal election saw 11 Indigenous people elected to the Commonwealth Parliament, representing a substantial and talented representation of the country's Indigenous population. Doesn't this represent the best possible Indigenous 'voice' to the Commonwealth Parliament?* [20]

The creation of a separate racialist group to have a "voice" in Parliament engenders distinctions that could eventually poison entire inter-cultural relationships.[21] Surely this could tempt some people to 'play the race card' that further aggravates existing legal-socio-cultural differences between Aboriginal Australians and all the other Australians.[22] For example, what might co-parenting a child be like when one parent is deemed more legitimate than the other in the eyes of the law simply because of his/her culture or skin-colour?

The entrenchment of the Voice in the Constitution will engender further difficulties where Aboriginal culture must be defined. This includes the possible acceptance as "cultural" of behaviour which otherwise would not be necessarily tolerated.[23] As observed by Gary Johns, a former Labor MP and minister in the Keating

20 Peter Kurti and Nyunggai Warren Mundine, 'Introduction: On Reconsidering The Voice to Parliament', in Peter Kurti and Warren Mundine AO, *Beyond Belief: Rethinking the Voice to Parliament* (Connor Court Publishing, 2022)

21 Kerryn Pholi, 'Upsetting the Intermarriage Applecart', *in* Gary Johns (ed.) *Recognise What? Arguments to Acknowledge Aboriginal Culture or Rights in the Australian Constitution* (Connor Court, 2014) 63.

22 Johns, n. 10, xvi.

23 Gary Johns, 'Already Recognition Enough', *in* Gary Johns (ed.) *Recognise What? Arguments to Acknowledge Aboriginal Culture or Rights, in the Australian Constitution* (Connor Court, 2014) 29.

government, "some Aboriginal elders and, following their lead, recent government enquiries into child sexual abuse, having found bad behaviour among Aborigines, make a leap to the refuge of 'culture' to solve the problem".[24] Accordingly, the practice of placing Aboriginal children in need of care with "culturally appropriate" carers have on many occasions ended in tragedy. According to Anthony Dillon, an academic lecturer who identifies himself as a 'part-Aboriginal Australian',

> *Some children have suffered, all in the name of "culture". A colour-blind culture or way of life, characterised by love is a far more important consideration than a culture that is assumed to be Aboriginal simply because the adult potential carers themselves have some Aboriginal ancestry.*[25]

The Voice is, at heart, a transfer of power that shifts power from Parliament to a race-based body that would be constitutionally empowered to make 'representations' not merely about proposed legislation but also about any act or omission to the parliament, or the government, or any of its agencies.[26] Despite insisting that the Voice will be merely "advisory", as the Prime Minister has candidly admitted, it would have to be a "very brave" government to not accept its "advice".[27] According to Janet Albrechtsen,

> *The Voice will create constant opportunities for a tiny minority of activists to hold parliament and executive government to ransom by using the immense leverage and opportunities for lawfare carefully woven into the [proposed] Amendment. It is not exaggeration to say it will cause the*

24 Johns, n. 10, 99.

25 Dillon, n. 17, 55.

26 Janet Albrechtsen, 'The Voice: Beyond Belief?', in Peter Kurti and Warren Mundine AO, *Beyond Belief: Rethinking the Voice to Parliament* (Connor Court Publishing, 2022) 32

27 Tony Abbott, 'The Voice: A Plea to Reconsider', in Peter Kurti and Warren Mundine AO, *Beyond Belief: Rethinking the Voice to Parliament* (Connor Court Publishing, 2022) 7

> *end of parliamentary democracy as we have known it.*[28]

Above all, the campaign for the Voice is not just about alleged Aboriginal rights. Objectively speaking, Aborigines presently do not lack any legal rights and their primary struggle is with the ingrained habits incentivised by government policies that prevent some from getting a foothold in the Australian economy. Following a successful amendment what must comprise any such "Aboriginal rights" automatically becomes a matter of constitutional interpretation for the High Court to decide. Since unelected judges are part of a ruling class that is not directly accountable to the electorate, they are more likely than politicians to give a small number of activists what they want.[29] And yet, as Keith Windschuttle points out,

> *Most constitutional critics today regard democracy not as an objective they must pursue but an obstacle they must overcome. For them, it is democracy that is the problem because it gives the majority of ordinary Australians the last word in deciding who governs. In the eyes of those who now dominate our cultural institutions and much of our political leadership, most ordinary Australians are uneducated, uncouth, racist rednecks, and a Constitution that gives people like them such power is unbearably frustrating.*[30]

Having been a legal academic in Australia for more than two decades, and having served for many years as a law reform commissioner in Western Australia, allow me to openly state that my interactions with the "political class and cultural elite" confirm the veracity of Windschuttle's statement. Indeed, the ruling classes in this country have a vested interest in fomenting a divisive

28 Albrechtsen, n. 26, 15.

29 Keith Windschuttle, *The Break-up of Australia: The Real Agenda Behind Aboriginal Recognition* (Quadrant Books, 2016) 15.

30 Ibid. 423.

racialist agenda that seriously undermines political equality. Their primary goal is not social amelioration of the Aboriginal condition but rather to gain a once-in-a-lifetime opportunity to substantially alter the Constitution in order to fulfil their own political ambitions.[31] As Senator Jacinta Nampijinpa Price put it, this is about dividing Australia along racial lines by entrenching indigenous separatism and constitutionally enshrining "the idea that Aboriginal people are perpetual victims forever in the need of special measures".[32]

### 4. Establishment of Religion?

On becoming Prime Minister in May 2023, Anthony Albanese promised to implement the *Uluru Statement from the Heart* in full.[33] "On Behalf of the Australian Labor Party, I commit to the Uluru Statement from the Heart in Full", he said on 21 May, moments after winning the federal election.[34]

The Uluru Statement encompasses a Voice to Parliament and Government, truth telling, treaty and some form of Aboriginal sovereignty or self-government. The Voice – an advisory body of "First Nations people" to Parliament – "aims to change the course of Australia's parliament" and is the first and enabling step to these other demands.[35]

31 Ibid.

32 Senator Jacinta Nampijinpa Price, 'The Voice Sunds Too Good to be True", in Peter Kurti and Warren Mundine AO, *Beyond Belief: Rethinking the Voice to Parliament* (Connor Court Publishing, 2022) xi.

33 'Read Incoming Prime Minister Anthony Albanese's Full Speech After Labor Wins Federal Election', *ABC News*, 21 May 2022, at https://www.abc.net.au/news/2022-05-22/anthony-albanese-acceptance-speech-full-transcript/101088736.

34 'Uluru Statement from the Heart's Voice Aims to Change the Course of Australia's Parliament. Here's How', *SBS News*, 18 August 2023, at https://www.sbs.com.au/news/article/uluru-statement-from-the-hearts-voice-aims-to-change-the-course-of-australias-parliament-heres-how/xhkpdrget.

35 Ibid.

Geoff Scott, former executive officer to the Referendum Council established in 2015 by then prime minister Malcolm Turnbull, told SBS News that "the Voice will help shape all bills and laws in Australia, it'll more specifically play a pivotal role in scrutinising legislation that directly affects First Nations communities".[36] Similarly, Marcia Langton, the co-chair of a senior advisory group of the Voice's design process, believes that "the proposed First Nations advisory body will aim to get involved in the "policy process from the beginning". "We propose that the Voice give advice to the government when requested and also when the members of the Voice think it's important to do so," Professor Langton said.[37]

As can be seen, proponents of the Voice tend to condone a violation of the principle of equality before the law so as to atone for the alleged systemic violations of equality in the past. And yet, they fail to explain how it is possible to correct any past discrimination by ultimately condoning the entrenchment in the Australian Constitution of a race-base system that directly violates the egalitarian principle of equal treatment of all citizens.

The idea of equality before the law in western democracies is traditionally derived from the Christian view of the equality of all individuals in the sight of God. St Paul's words in his Letter to the Galatians, "the ultimate Christian statement of the inherent dignity of each person", make the principle of equality an uncompromising position: "There is neither Jew nor Greek, neither bond nor free, nor is there male and female, given you are one in Christ Jesus".[38] It is this sentiment that directly motivated the American Declaration of Independence and its famous statement:

> *We hold these truths to be self-evident, that all men are*

36 Ibid.

37 Ibid.

38 Galatians 3:28.

> *created equal, that they are endowed by their Creator with certain unalienable Rights, that among these are Life, Liberty and the pursuit of Happiness.*

The statement of equality expressed in this Declaration refers to the axiom that we are all members of the same human race because we are all created in the image of God.[39] This view of the inherent dignity of every person is an inheritance which is carved into the very foundations of western constitutionalism.[40] Hence, when speaking at the Australasian constitutional convention, Patrick Glynn of South Australia contended that it was to the nation's credit that it had the stamp of Christianity "fixed upon the front of our institutions."[41]

Indeed, the Commonwealth of Australia was initially understood "to be the work of human hands and the invisible hand of God".[42] The preamble, that part in the Constitution which lays out the hopes and aspiration of all the parties involved, communicates that the Australian people, "humbly relying on the blessing of Almighty God, ha[d] agreed to unite in one indissoluble Federal Commonwealth". Constitutional law professor Helen Irving explains that, in that time, this acknowledgement of God received the strongest popular support of *any* part of the Australian Constitution.[43]

---

39 Harry V. Jaffa, Equality and Liberty (Claremont, 1999), 177-8. Quoted from Hadley Arkes, *Natural Rights and the Right to Choose* (New York/NY: Cambridge University Press, 2002) 45.

40 The Reverend Robert Sirico, 'How Will Freedom Succeed?', *Robert H. Krieble lecture delivered on April 24, 2008, at the 31st annual meeting of The Heritage Foundation Resource Bank in Atlanta/GO*, available at https://www.heritage.org/political-process/report/how-will-freedom-succeed

41 5 *Official Record of the Debates of the Australasian Federal Convention* 1733 (1898) (proceedings of March 2, 1898).

42 Anthony G. Percy, *Australia: What Went Right? What Went Wrong?* (Connor Court Publishing, 2022) 72.

43 Helen Irving, *To Constitute a Nation: A Cultural History of Australia's Constitution* (Cambridge University Press, 1999) 196.

An overriding concern among the constitutional framers was to draft a document that prevented the new federal government from establishing monopolies and concentrating too much power. One of the most significant issues facing Australians in that period was that of managing religious pluralism.[44] This attitude guided the framers as they drafted Section 116 of the Constitution, dealing with religious life. Remember that our Constitution originated in a social environment with different branches of the Christian church competing for cultural influence. It is against this background that Section 116, which the U.S. Constitution's First Amendment obviously inspired, must be interpreted:

> *The Commonwealth shall not make any law for establishing any religion, or for imposing any religious observance, or for prohibiting the free exercise of any religion, and no religious test shall be required as qualification for any office or public trust under the Commonwealth.*[45]

This important provision contains several prohibitions: first, the establishment of religion; second, the imposition of any requirement to engage in religious rituals; third, any law preventing the free exercise of religion; and fourth, the imposition of religious qualifications for public office. In other words, no official religion and compulsion in religion.

But this is when the Voice proposal becomes even more problematic. A First Nations Voice to Parliament protected by the Constitution is a key element of the *Uluru Statement from the Heart*.[46] And yet, just after stating that the Indigenous tribes "were the first sovereign Nations of the Australian continent", the Statement goes on to state the following:

---

44 Peter Kurti, 'Religion and the New Sectarianism: Countering the Call for Silence', in James Allan (ed.), *Making Australia Right: Where to from Here?* (Redland Bay/Qld: Connor Court Publishing, 2016) 171.

45 *Constitution of the Commonwealth of Australia 1900* (Cth) s 116.

46 'The Uluru Statement', at https://ulurustatement.org/

> *This sovereignty is a spiritual notion: the ancestral tie between the land, or 'mother nature', and the Aboriginal and Torres Strait Islander peoples who were born therefrom, remain attached thereto, and must one day return thither to be united with our ancestors. This link is the basis of the ownership of the soil, or better, of sovereignty.*

The religious foundations in such a claim for Aboriginal sovereignty can hardly be denied. The spiritual bond that the writers say gives the Aboriginal and Torres Strait Islander peoples a sovereign claim on the land is a religious statement that explicitly articulates nature worship and ancestor worship. The writers speak of sovereignty as a spiritual notion associated with "the ancestral tie between the land, or 'mother nature', and the Aboriginal and Torres Strait Islander peoples who were born therefrom, remain attached thereto, and must one day return thither to be united with our ancestors".

The Voice proposal is based on, and inspired by, this particular religious statement. It is thus necessary to consider the religious dimension of the proposed entrenchment of the 'Voice' to Parliament as per the 'Uluru Statement From The Heart', which must be considered in light of Section 116 of the Australian Constitution that prohibits any establishment of religion. According to Gabriël A. Moens, "the Government's unqualified adoption and implementation of the Statement and its tenacious promotion of the Voice could thus be characterised as an establishment of religion in Australia and the imposition of religious observance on people in society".[47]

47 See Chapter 2.

## 5. Concluding Comments

The Government's tenacious promotion of the 'Indigenous Voice' to parliament can be described as an attempt to establish a religious observance in the form of Aboriginal spirituality. Those who aspire to serve on the 'Voice' to parliament will need to qualify as ardent proponents of the Uluru Statement From the Heart. However, such Statement effectively establishes a form of religion that articulates nature worship and ancestor worship. The writers speak of sovereignty as a spiritual notion based on the ancestral tie between the land, or "mother nature". This directly violates the constitutional directive found in Section 116 that no religious test shall be used to determine the suitability of people for government positions.

One of the great virtues of our Constitution is its equal treatment of all citizens. Far from being "racist" this document is entirely colour-blind. It treats everyone equally, no matter when they or their ancestors arrived here. It is therefore entirely inappropriate to use this document to promote one group over the rest of the population.[48] Accordingly, enshrining the Voice in the Australian Constitution will create political inequality and perpetuate divisiveness.[49] Thus, at a philosophical level, the Voice proposal is profoundly illiberal, divisive and inequitable since "it creates permanent race-based privilege and turns Australia into a constitutionally endorsed two-tier society".[50]

Ultimately, enshrining the Voice in the Constitution will "lead us down that dark corridor on the basis of race – thus prolonging

48 Wesley Aird, 'Recognition is Blackfella Politics', in Gary Johns (ed.) *Recognise What? Arguments to Acknowledge Aboriginal Culture or Right, in the Australian Constitution* (Connor Court, 2014), 49.

49 Samuelson, , n. 8, 68.

50 Albrechtsen, n. 26, 15.

the sorry history of racial difference".[51] Perhaps this is actually the hidden agenda of the ruling classes: to further divide us into lines of culture, origin and ethnicity so as to facilitate the attainment of more power and control. Indeed, some people may have a vested interest in fomenting a socially divisive agenda that further undermines political equality and turns fellow Australians against each other. This is basically a revisitation of the "divide and conquer" strategy so successfully applied by the ancient Romans.

51 Henry Ergas AO, 'The Voice in the Light of the Western Intellectual Tradition', in: Peter Kurti and Warren Mundine AO, *Beyond Belief: Rethinking the Voice to Parliament* (Connor Court Publishing, 2022) 155.

# 4

# CONSTITUTIONAL RECOGNITION OF ABORIGINAL AND TORRES STRAIT ISLANDER PEOPLES

**Bob Gregory***

*"Behold, how good and how pleasant it is for brethren to dwell together in unity!"*[1]

One of the great features of us Aussies, for which we have become renowned around the world, is our tendency to champion the underdog and our collective cry for a "fair go!" As a cosmopolitan, eclectic culture, it is one of the great unifying factors of our country and, one might say, is the spirit that will shape the way a majority of our population votes in the forthcoming referendum to recognise our Aboriginal and Torres Strait Islander peoples in the Australian Constitution.

Australian people, historically, have been very wary when it comes to changing their Constitution. It is a foundational document

* Rev Dr Bob Gregory is a retired Pastor and Christian School Principal. He was a founder of Providence Christian College in Southern River, WA and was then appointed as Managing Director of a Christian Curriculum company, based in Brisbane. In 2006 Bob was nominated as the CPA Australian Business Leader of the Year.

1 Psalm 133:1 NKJV.

which ought to provide the governing principles behind every legislative, administrative, and public service action within the nation. Quite rightly, its alteration should only be proposed rarely, with great care and for the right reasons.

Above all, the Constitution must be a tool to foster unity and a "fair go" amongst this diverse, multicultural population of Australia, as much as that is possible. The Government of the day, of whatever flavour they may be, has the unenviable task of implementing the Constitution for the benefit of all of the nation's people. A major part of this obligation is to make laws aimed at fostering harmony and unity within the populace.

So, is there a need for this proposed amendment?

It would be instructive, prior to addressing that question, to turn our minds to some of the history that has made our Constitution, and our nation, what it is today. There was a time when our Aboriginal people were expressly excluded from recognition within the Constitution and were barred from being counted in the national census.

In 1967 the Australian population was asked, in a referendum, to correct this error and overwhelmingly (with a 90.77% majority) voted to remove racial recognition from the Constitution. This was consistent with the eradication of the "White Australia Policy" by the Holt government the previous year (1966). Australia, with the decisive approval of the people, was moving towards a more inclusive, tolerant nation, welcoming of all cultures, nationalities, and races.

This was the spiritual temperature of the nation at that time. The majority of our population identified as Christian and were keen to put into practice the injunctions of Scripture, such as that found in Leviticus; *"The stranger who dwells among you shall be to you as one born among you, and you shall love him as yourself; for you were strangers in the land of Egypt: I am the LORD your God."*[2]

Whilst our Aboriginal peoples were already here at the arrival of the First Fleet, the rest of us came from somewhere else! Indeed, even our Indigenous people came from elsewhere, in the distant past. Our national "heart" is that we all be treated the same, that we all have a "fair go," and that we all partake in the bounty of the wonderful continent we share together.

Our friends from across the Tasman have their own experience of an equivalent to "The Voice". "New Zealand's failed Māori Voice to Parliament, the Waitangi Tribunal, which the Prime Minister held up as a model for Australia, has imposed dangerous policies that put a person's race above all other considerations in government decision making," said John Storey, Research Fellow at the Institute of Public Affairs."[3]

So, will the proposed "Voice to Parliament" become a further unifying factor, or will it become a fulcrum upon which division and contention become permanently enshrined within our Nation? Having once crushingly vetoed the recognition of race in the Constitution, for the very purpose of creating more harmony, acceptance, and tolerance in our society, would its reinstatement now be more likely to embed division, strife, and rejection within the community? The answer to that question largely depends on how "The Voice" is worded, how it is interpreted and how it is administered.

The current wording, and it would seem that this is now settled, is problematic on two main fronts. Firstly, it is extremely vague and can be interpreted to mean almost anything. Secondly, it does not accomplish anything that is not already available to the Indigenous population, either in the Constitution or in Parliament.

---

2 Leviticus 19:34 (NKJV)

3 At https://ipa.org.au/ipa-today/new-zealands-failed-experiment-highlights-voice-to--parliament-dangers

On the first point, it could be argued that interpretation of the wording is the prerogative of the Government alone and is therefore in "safe hands." Governments, however, are notorious for using ambiguous language to run agendas that can turn out to be very different to that implied by the original wording. It was Ronald Reagan, $40^{th}$ President of the United States of America, who famously said; "The nine most terrifying words in the English language are: 'I'm from the government and I'm here to help.'" Reagan knew, as did John F Kennedy before him, that unbridled authority leads to unhealthy outcomes. Both suffered assassination attempts, successful in the case of JFK, because they dared to attempt correcting the challenges that had arisen within their governmental structure.

The Prime Minister's statement that he would not introduce legislation on a proposed model for the Indigenous voice until after the Constitutional Referendum is provocative, and an indication he is concerned that doing so would, in fact, harm the "yes" campaign. It would be naïve, to suggest the Australian people simply trust that the outcome will be equitable.

For the wording of "The Voice" to have no mention of process, no inclusion of control mechanisms and neither a sunset clause, nor a means of removal, ought to raise red flags in any rational mind. We need to ask, and have definitively answered, questions such as: How will candidates be selected? By what mechanism will they present their proposals to Parliament, and what responsibility will Parliament have for the recommendations they make? Does enshrining "The Voice" in our Constitution have any ramifications on our international obligations (for example, through the United Nations Declaration on The Rights of Indigenous Peoples)? Should "The Voice" become redundant, or worse, begin to operate in a manner against the best interest of Australia as a whole, what redress do the Australian people have? Until such questions are answered, in a manner as final and permanent as a constitutional amendment, the people of Australia would indeed be foolhardy to vote "Yes"!

What is of equal or greater concern, addressing the second point, is that our Aboriginal and Torres Strait Islander people already have full protection under the current Constitution. Chapter 1, Part V, Section 51 (xxvi) confers upon Parliament the power to make laws with respect to; "the people of any race for whom it is deemed necessary to make special laws".[4] What is the need to add an amendment that would not increase its power or authority? Is the Government so concerned that it might not legislate in the best interests of our Indigenous population that it needs an amendment to our Constitution to force it to do so? Unlikely indeed!

Furthermore, with no less than eleven Indigenous Members in the current Parliament, this cohort of our society is already proportionally overrepresented. Added to that is the Prime Minister's Aboriginal advisory body, the Indigenous Advisory Council (IAC) established by then Prime Minister Tony Abbott, and The National Indigenous Australians Agency (NIAA) which have all of the benefits and none of the potential downfalls, of this proposed Constitutional amendment. One might ask, with the existing level of representation our Indigenous folk enjoy, why is the Government so keen to enshrine this "Voice" into the Constitution? Is there some concealed agenda? On the evidence gathered from credible sources, including our Indigenous people themselves, it would seem this may well be the case.

The mere fact that there is such critical division amongst our Aboriginal Australians in regard to "The Voice" ought to give the average Aussie pause for careful consideration. Were it, indeed, a "voice" for the collective Indigenous community, surely it is something they would collectively welcome. The strident

4 Part V - Powers of the Parliament – Parliament of Australia (aph.gov.au).

voices raised in opposition to this initiative, however, must give the average Aussie serious cause for concern. Senator Jacinta Nampijinpa Price, part of the Warlpiri group, stated during the Parliamentary inquiry into the Uluru Declaration, that neither she nor her people were consulted regarding "The Voice", a claim echoed by many other Indigenous leaders.

Does this mean, then, that the Uluru Declaration From the Heart, the event which gave birth to "The Voice", was a selected group representing only those with a vested interest in the outcome? Such is the claim made by many people who have a keen interest in that outcome.

According to Senator Matt O'Sullivan, who recently returned from a visit to the Kimberley in Western Australia, "It's clear to me that the model that's been proposed, it won't actually give these communities a voice. It'll be isolated in Canberra and will turn into yet another bureaucracy that frankly, these communities don't need.

"Now I've heard the desperation of these communities, and frankly, they're sick of bureaucracies ignoring their local wisdom. They want Local, State and Federal Governments to take them seriously – to implement programmes that will appropriately address their needs."[5]

Stephen Reason claims: "Their multifarious voices will be muted and reduced to a singular controlled Voice; and, consequently, a token "Aboriginal Parliament" will speak on their collective behalf."[6]

In any relationship, and one might argue there is no more important relationship, outside of that with our Creator, than that

5 At https://www.facebook.com/OSullivanWA/videos/924135705512591

6 At https://stephenreason.substack.com/p/the-real-agenda-behind-the-voice?utm_source=direct&utm_campaign=post&utm_medium=web

of a nation with their government, there needs to be a triumvirate of interrelated factors: Truth, Transparency, and Trust.

In the Gospel of John, Jesus said; *"For everyone practicing evil hates the light and does not come to the light, lest his deeds should be exposed. But he who does the truth comes to the light, that his deeds may be clearly seen, that they have been done in God."*[7]

Truth must be accompanied by transparency. These two factors are foundational to the building of trust. For any government to have a trust relationship with the people of their nation, there must be both truth and transparency.

An example of the failure of government to operate transparently with the Australian people was set by our previous Prime Minister Scott Morrison who, without consultation with his own party, let alone the population, installed himself clandestinely (along with a raft of other ministries) as Treasurer alongside Josh Frydenberg. Apparently, he did this with the primary purpose of controlling the Foreign Investment Review Boad (FIRB).

Whilst in this capacity, Prime Minister Morrison approved the foreign acquisition of Australian infrastructure to the tune of AU$131 billion, as against AU$33 billion the previous year. Amongst the fire sale of Aussie assets were Australia's gateway, Sydney Airport, which was snapped up by a consortium of private equity funds led by Global Infrastructure Partners for AU$24 bn. Energy giant Ausnet went to Brookfield for AU$20 bn and energy provider Spark Infrastructure was sold to Kohlberg Kravis Roberts and the Ontario Teachers' Pension Fund for AU$ 5.2 bn.[8]

What is most concerning about these deals is that, whilst it seems Mr Morrison had himself secretly installed as Finance Minister

---

7 John 3:20-21 (NKJV).

8 At https://michaelwest.com.au/a-royal-commission-into-scott-morrison-he-sold-off-the-farm-in-secret/.

in order to facilitate their approval, the transactions themselves did not take place in a vacuum. Other government members and non-elected administrative bureaucrats in Canberra knew of these deals, yet the public at large, to whom these assets rightfully belonged, was neither credibly consulted, nor informed.

As these sales have already taken place, and triggered no alarm bells amongst the general Australian population, it raises the question, "How much of Australia is up for sale, and what are the consequences for the Australian people?" Whilst some may label it "Conspiracy Theory", and others simply dismiss it as conjecture, there is a very real and present danger to the Australian people concealed within this proposed "Voice to Parliament".

According to Steve Jeffery, of *Just One Focus – Truth,* "The 'Voice to Parliament' is a gift akin to the gigantic wooden horse once wheeled within the unsuspecting walls of ill-fated Troy. If we accept it, if we welcome it into our chambers of Parliament — it will destroy all from the inside."

The UN Declaration on The Rights of Indigenous Peoples (UNDRIP) — advises pursuing 'collective rights to land, territories and resources' for the Indigenous of 80% of Australian Land (but there will be no private land rights for anyone).[9]

The world's largest hard-rock lithium mine, the Greenbushes mine, is in Western Australia. It is co-operated by the Chinese company Tianiqi Lithium and the Australian companies Talison Lithium and IGO Limited. In 2021, it contributed 40% of the lithium mined in Australia.

In June, 2015, Australia's largest Native Title settlement (320,000 hectares of Crown land) was re-allocated to a Noongar Land Estate in Western Australia.

9 At https://www.justonefocus.org/this-is-war-how-the-voice-will-be-used-for-the-globalist-invasion-of-australia/.

"Forty-six per cent of the world's lithium (essential for the Green Energy agenda of electric vehicles and battery powered households) was mined from Western Australia in 2020. Tellingly, the world's largest lithium mine just happens to fall within the Noongar Land Estate region. Should the Voice be recognised in Parliament, a Treaty will gift this Native Title Land to the Transnational Corporatocracy and advocate for the establishment of more lithium mines (as The Voice will speak on behalf of all the "Indigenous" everywhere, always, and only to benefit the Corporatocracy.)"[10]

Josephine Cashman is a former Crown prosecutor, a lawyer and businesswoman with more than two decades of experience working towards economic progress for Aboriginal people. In 2013 to 17, she was a member of Prime Minister Tony Abbott's Indigenous Advisory Council. Josephine is one of the Indigenous people doing her best to alert Australians to the dangers hidden within this proposed constitutional amendment. She warns, "Globalists use "Indigenous" as a Device for a Worldwide Takeover."[11]

In the cited article, Josephine walks the reader through a carefully researched and logically presented process articulating her concerns associated with "The Voice" as it is proposed. In her article, Josephine demonstrates the extent to which these UN treaties are used around the world to transfer rights over the wealth of nations to the corporate conglomerates who fund (and control) them.

A "Yes" vote to this proposed "Voice" puts the nation at risk of a globalist takeover of the very land and resources that the most trusting of us think are being returned to their "rightful" owners. Is this likely to occur? We must conduct our own research, carefully

10 Ibid.

11 At https://josephinecashman.substack.com/p/globalists-use-indigenous-as-a-device.

consider the claims that are made, and weigh the evidence.

We must also ask ourselves, "Is there a need?" "Can the needs of our Indigenous population be met in another, less hazardous manner?" And "Has the government fulfilled its responsibility of Truth and Transparency in order to earn the Trust of the Australian people?"

You decide!

# 5

# A THEOLOGICAL ASSESSMENT OF "THE VOICE"

**Mark Powell***

## 1. Introduction: Christ and Culture

The life, death, resurrection, and ascension of Christ Jesus have fundamentally altered the course of human history. So much so that the Bible tells us that faith in the Son of God produces not only 'vertical' reconciliation between oneself and God the Father, but also 'horizontal' reconciliation between one another as people made in His image (Titus 3:3-8; Galatians 3:26-29; Ephesians 2:11-22). Wherever this message of 'good news' has been preached and practically applied, it has had—by the power of the Holy Spirit—a personally transforming and socially unifying effect.

The Voice to parliament though, seeks to proclaim a political solution to what is actually a spiritual problem. Indigenous religious practices such as those included in 'Makarrata' and 'The Uluru Statement from the Heart' (TUSH) are an attempt to replace the person and work of Christ with another gospel which is really no 'gospel' at all. And while it might promise prosperity and peace, The Voice will only perpetuate guilt, division, and spiritual syncretism. What's more, 'The Voice' will fail to achieve any real-world change for those in need.

---

* Mark Powell is the Teaching Elder at Cornerstone Presbyterian Community Church in Hobart.

I believe 'The Voice' undermines core Biblical doctrines such as creation, sin, atonement, and ultimately reconciliation between various groups of people. And because of this, 'The Voice' represents a clear and present danger by promoting indigenous spirituality and a path to reconciliation outside of the person and work of Christ.

2. **The Voice Will Undermine Equality and Entrench Division**

The first congregation I served in as an ordained minister in the Presbyterian Church of Australia was in North-West NSW, in a small town called Wee Waa, where a large proportion of the community were indigenous. During my seven years there, I observed numerous social problems including child sexual abuse, chronic unemployment, welfare dependency, domestic violence, alcohol and substance abuse, school truancy and youth crime. Sadly, as the Shadow Indigenous Minister, Jacinta Nampijinpa Price—as well as the indigenous leader Warren Mundine and academic Anthony Dillon—have all lamented, these problems continue to exist, especially in remote aboriginal communities.

Even though Aboriginal and Torres Strait Islander people share in $33 billion dollars of government welfare annually (over $20 billion in targeted assistance), 'The Voice' will fail to make the lives of most indigenous peoples any better—just like under ATSIC—except for a burgeoning bureaucratic indigenous class. Both TUSH and 'The Voice' draw from a wider socio-political philosophy pejoratively referred to as "wokeism", or the more increasingly recognized socio-political movement known as Cultural Marxism. While it is beyond the scope of this chapter to explore the subject in-depth, the following exchange by the atheist/ agnostic academics respectively, Peter Boghossian (PB) and James Lindsay (JL), are especially enlightening.

> *PB: I have had in the back of my mind that if this were at the height of the new atheist movement—and when we were extremely involved in that—if I wanted a plan, if I were going to design a plan to bring the whole thing down...*
>
> *JL: Yes, let's end Christianity, how do we do it?*
>
> *PB: All of Christendom, yeah, how would you do it?*
>
> *JL: Make them woke! Because it will eat itself from the inside. I'm not the old guard atheist that I alluded to earlier ... but if I were the old school angry atheist ... like, "Let's just throw rocks at the Cathedral until it falls down!" I'd start making woke pastors and sending them in, because they're going to tear everything apart. Because they're going to make everything about identity and that's all they'll ever talk about.*

The problem is that The Voice is inherently 'racist' because it assumes that all indigenous people have the same perspective on political issues, which is obviously, both demeaning and patronising. What's more, 'The Voice' propagates a form of paternalistic colonialism which it ironically claims to eradicate. True respect and democratic equality are established though, not by giving one particular group of people a 'voice' regarding their own affairs, but in them also being able to have a say in how the rest of the nation functions. As the Opposition Leader, Peter Dutton, has said in response to the government's proposal regarding The Voice:

> *It will have an Orwellian effect where* All Australians are equal, but some Australians are more equal than others. *This Voice, as proposed by the Prime Minister, promotes difference. And it's sadly a symptom of the madness of identity politics which has infected the 21st century. The Voice will re-racialise our nation. At a time when we need to unite*

> *the country, this Prime Minister's proposal will permanently divide us by race.*[1]

Thus, because The Voice will fundamentally divide indigenous and non-indigenous Australians against one another, it ultimately undermines the person and work of Christ, the message of the Christian Gospel which is to reconcile people from all nations to Almighty God (John 3:16; Revelation 5:1-14).

### 3. Some Political Background

Much of the present debate can be traced back to the Prime Ministership of John Howard who, while expressing personal sorrow for what had happened to Indigenous Australians in the past, refused to offer an official apology on behalf of the government. Significantly, Howard's position brought him into direct conflict with Peter Jensen, the then newly elected Anglican Archbishop of Sydney, who was widely reported in the media at the time as accusing the Prime Minister of "being out of step with God". While technically the Archbishop posed his comment as a question, Archbishop Jensen did say:

> *I think he is wrong ... I think he [Howard] has a view which, unfortunately, is not communal enough. I think his view is too individualistic and he should recognise the Christian understanding, which is that we belong together and we do things together and we have a joint responsibility for things.*[2]

Jensen's perspective may well have anticipated the ascendancy of identity politics, but what if the philosophical position of the politician (Howard) was more prescient than the prelate's (Jensen)?

---

1 At https://www.peterdutton.com.au/leader-of-the-opposition-transcript-constitution-alteration-aboriginal-and-torres-strait-islander-voice-2023-second-reading-speech-house-of-representatives/.

2 Andrew West, "Enough already!" *The Monthly,* December 2005-January 2006.

The reason I say this is because Howard wasn't arguing against the idea of corporate responsibility *per se* but whether or not individuals of the present generation should be held responsible for the actions of individuals in a previous generation's, namely the "sins of the fathers" (i.e. Exodus 20:5-6; 34:6-7; Numbers 14:18).

### 4. The Biblical Foundation for Repentance

What has been routinely overlooked in this debate so far, is not only the large amount of good the church has done for indigenous people since European settlement, but any discussion of passages of Scripture which teach that only the soul who is guilty of sin should be punished. Take, for instance, the passage found in Ezekiel 18:

> *But suppose this son has a son who sees all the sins his father commits, and though he sees them, he does not do such things: "He does not eat at the mountain shrines or look to the idols of Israel. He does not defile his neighbour's wife. He does not oppress anyone or require a pledge for a loan. He does not commit robbery but gives his food to the hungry and provides clothing for the naked. He withholds his hand from mistreating the poor and takes no interest or profit from them. He keeps my laws and follows my decrees. He will not die for his father's sin; he will surely live. But his father will die for his own sin, because he practiced extortion, robbed his brother and did what was wrong among his people. "Yet you ask, 'Why does the son not share the guilt of his father?' Since the son has done what is just and right and has been careful to keep all my decrees, he will surely live. The one who sins is the one who will die. The child will not share the guilt of the parent, nor will the parent share the guilt of the child. The righteousness of the righteous will be credited to them, and*

> *the wickedness of the wicked will be charged against them.*[3]

Significantly, Anglican theologians such as Drs Michael Jensen and Peter Adam assume the legitimacy of intergenerational guilt. This leads them to conclude that non-indigenous Australians today, even recently arrived migrants who are refugees and have been born two-hundred years since the first white settlement in Australia, and did not participate in any crimes of theft, murder or covetousness, are morally culpable. Nevertheless, Jensen and Adam believe they benefit from the practice of colonialism and therefore share in the same spiritual guilt. As Jensen states:

> *And lest we say 'we' have not done anything of the kind, we should as readers of Scripture acknowledge the reality of intergenerational culpability; or if not; the responsibility we have as fellow citizens to reckon with the injustices of the past which have not as yet been resolved (and, to repeat, from which we benefit).*[4]

Following on from this, Adam argues that we should "ask the indigenous people if they wanted those of us who have arrived since 1788 to leave"! The theological problem with this position though, is that Adam and Jensen fail to engage with the teaching of passages such as Ezekiel 18, even though they are aware of its truth.

Unfortunately, even the Sydney Anglican Diocesan Doctrine Commission (SADDC), chaired by Dr Mark Thompson, also avoids the teaching of Ezekiel 18. In a recent resource paper titled, 'A Theological Framework for Reconciliation: With Special Reference to The Indigenous Peoples of Australia', it states:

> *... like other communities, organisations in the abstract have a continuity with the past which individual members do not,*

3 Ezekiel 18:14-20.

4 Michael Jensen, *The Voice: A Christian Consideration* (Unpublished Paper), 5.

> *and this puts them in a position to take responsibility for the sins of the fathers, and make restitution for those who continue to suffer from past wrongs.*

However, the doctrinal position of Jensen, Adam, and the SADDC is at odds with key passages of Scripture such as Jeremiah 31 and especially Ezekiel 18. These texts teach that children should *not* be punished for the sins of their fathers. Moreover, they are also in danger of making the same error of the disciples when they asked Jesus in John 9 whether it was a man's parents or his own sin which was the reason he was born blind.

## 5. The Problem of the Heart

Integral to the referendum question involving 'The Voice' is obviously the place of the 'heart'. This implicitly calls for a compassionate response from the hearer, lest they be labelled as being 'heartless'. Significantly, Kanishka Raffel, the present Anglican Archbishop of Sydney, wrote in an article in support of TUSH for *The Australian*:

> *That it was made "from the heart" has particular resonance for Christians like me. In the Bible Jesus speaks often of the power and significance of the heart. In warning against greed and challenging our priorities, Jesus said, "For where your treasure is, there your heart will be also", or in another place, "out of the abundance of the heart the mouth speaks."*[5]

However, the Archbishop's argument doesn't really do justice as to how the term "heart" is used throughout the Bible. Yes, the heart can be a vehicle for expressing desire or emotion, but that is not always a good thing. This is because a person's heart has been corrupted by sin and as such, is an unreliable guide. As the

5 Kanishka Raffel, "Walking together on journey from the heart", *The Australian.* May 31, 2022.

prophet Jeremiah says, "The heart is deceitful above all things and beyond cure. Who can understand it?" (Jeremiah 17:9) In contrast, the fifth and sixth paragraphs of TUSH state:

> *Proportionally, we are the most incarcerated people on the planet. We are not an innately criminal people. Our children are aliened from their families at unprecedented rates. This cannot be because we have no love for them. And our youth languish in detention in obscene numbers. They should be our hope for the future.*
>
> *These dimensions of our crisis tell plainly the structural nature of our problem. This is the torment of our powerlessness. (Italics original)*

While the statement that "we are the most incarcerated people on the planet" is somewhat contested, factors other than 'systemic racism'—i.e. such as absent fathers, chronic welfare dependency and substance abuse—are surely more sociologically significant. This is because, according to the Australian Bureau of Statistics, since Kevin Rudd made a formal 'apology' to indigenous people on the 13 February 2008, criminal acts intended to cause injury, as well as sexual assault and related offences amongst indigenous peoples have continued to rise.

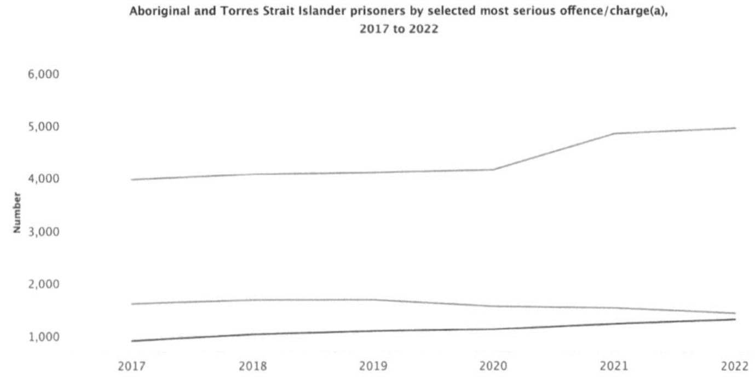


(a) For a definition of most serious offence/charge, see Methodology, Most serious offence/charge section.

Source: Australian Bureau of Statistics, Prisoners in Australia 2022

Are indigenous people saying that they have no personal agency for their situation and that their high rates of incarnation are because they lack political power? Even more seriously, are indigenous people saying the reason they are being arrested is simply because of their race? Or is family breakdown, substance abuse, violent crime and the subsequent incarceration rates a result of the spiritual brokenness which we all wrestle with as fallen human beings?

### 6. Enshrining Spirituality into the Constitution

A key aspect in the present debate which has been largely overlooked involves the separation of Church and State. Although recently, Constitutional legal experts such as Augusto Zimmermann and Gabriël Moens have pointed out:

> *In the case of the Uluru Statement From The Heart, the religious foundations of the 'Voice' based on 'sovereignty' as a 'spiritual notion' can hardly be denied. Such Statement is clearly a religious document because it explicitly articulates nature worship and ancestor worship.*
>
> *The writers of this Statement speak of Aboriginal sovereignty in terms of 'a spiritual notion: the ancestral tie between the land, or 'mother nature', and the Aboriginal and Torres Strait Islander peoples who were born therefrom, remain attached thereto, and must one day return thither to be united with our ancestors'.*
>
> *It is this spiritual bond that the writers say gives them claim on the land.*
>
> *It is thus time to consider the religious dimension of the proposed entrenchment of the 'Voice' to Parliament as per the 'Uluru Statement from the Heart', which must be considered*

> *particularly in light of Section 116 of the Australian Constitution that prohibits any establishment of religion.*[6]

This emphasis is evidenced by TUSH's use of indigenous 'dreaming' iconography in its artistic presentation of the document, and the religious understanding of reconciliation as the proposed by the Makarrata Commission. The question can reasonably be asked "Is The Voice in contradiction to Section 116 of the Australian Constitution which states, "The Commonwealth should not make any law for establishing any religion or for imposing any religious observance"'? While the wording of 'The Voice' does not argue for the establishment of a religion *per se,* its advocates clearly see it as fulfilling a spiritual void. As Noel Pearson, has said:

> *There's an emptiness there. It's like we haven't found our heart.*
>
> *Now is the time to pull it together to achieve recognition in the nation's most supreme legal document, which is the Constitution. So, constitutional recognition answers a spiritual need in the Australian nation. (emphasis added).*[7]

While most modern indigenous practices are tokenistic—e.g. a 'Welcome to Country' has to be extended as well as listened too and received—these animistic religious practices were traditionally observed by indigenous groups before European settlement as a way of providing spiritual 'safe passage' through a neighbouring territory. Hence, as Michael Murphy from Sydney University rightly argues, "...it becomes apparent that when participating in a contemporary Welcome to Country (WtC) those who are present enter into a public prayer which reverences the Aboriginal

6 Gabriël Moens & Augusto Zimmerman, "Does the Uluru Statement from the Heart violate the Constitution? *The Spectator Australia,* 24 April 2023.

7 Quoted in Troy Bramston, "Pearson rues former PM's missteps", *The Weekend Australian,* 28 April 2023.

ontological understanding of Country".[8] What's more, according to Murphy, this is because of three foundational Indigenous religious truths:

1. Through the continuation of the Dreaming narrative, Indigenous people practice their religion's intrinsic metaphysic, linked to the land both spatially and temporally.
2. Aboriginals of different nations fundamentally respect and understand the religious traditions of other nations when historically engaging in a Welcome to Country.
3. The Elders are the custodians or magisterium of the sacred tradition.

In a similar way to WtC, 'Acknowledgement of Country' (AoC) involves recognising the timeless presence of indigenous elders past, present and emerging. Thus, unlike the Western act of "remembrance"—associated with events such as ANZAC day—the indigenous religious ritual of AoC is a form of 'ancestor worship'. In this sense, a good parallel example is the Asian practice of honouring departed relatives at their graves each year.

The Australian Parliament is already opened annually with an indigenous smoking ceremony—a form of cleansing and protection from evil spirits—and the indigenous religious rituals of WtC and AoC are now virtually ubiquitous. However, if 'The Voice' is enshrined into the Constitution, then we can expect the observance of these pantheistic religious practices to be promoted politically and possibly even mandated legally.

8 Michael Murphy, 'The Welcome to and Acknowledgement of Country in Australian Parliament', *Literature & Aesthetics* Vol. 29, No. 2 (2019), 128. Murphy concludes, "The sacred emerges as a prayer amongst the civic". 128.

### 7. Conclusion: The 'Heart' Should Not Overrule the 'Head'

Christians have a message of reconciliation which has the power to achieve what TUSH and The Voice never could. The person and work of Christ Jesus is the means to tear down the dividing wall of hostility not only *vertically* between us and God, but also *horizontally* between those from every tribe and nation (See Eph. 2). However, voting in favour of 'The Voice' introduces a political solution when the problem is fundamentally spiritual.

Christians should not only resist counterfeit political solutions but—in keeping with our nation's strong evangelical heritage—continue to humbly proclaim the Gospel of reconciliation to people from every nation, tribe and tongue (Matt. 28:19-20). In short, the human 'heart' must never overrule Christ as the 'head'. As the apostle Paul writes:

> *And he is the head of the body, the church; he is the beginning and the firstborn from among the dead, so that in everything he might have supremacy. For God was pleased to have all his fullness dwell in him, and through him to reconcile all things on earth or things in heaven, by making peace through his blood, shed on the cross. (Col. 1:18-20)*

# 6

# THE VOICE – A PEACEMAKER'S PARADIGM

**Neil Johnson***

One caller to my talk-radio program 20Twenty drew an insightful contrast between our Australian referendum for 'The Voice', to the 1990's South African movement to end apartheid. It too was a race-based referendum (2002). A question was put to the South African nation to establish whether every person should have the right to vote with a view to a negotiated process creating a new equality between black and white. South Africans voted for a reform process where everybody in a unified, multiracial South Africa would be treated equally with built in protections for minorities.[1] A groundswell of opinion is now asking if our Australian question risks an opposite result. Even the most modest inclusion of wording that differentiates our pre-existent united oneness as an Australian nation, risks a new era of permanent division based on ancestry and skin colour.

There are only two choices, YES or NO! Already, the campaign division is heated. The political messaging says choose one side, demonise the other. To vote No = 'racist,' to vote Yes = 'ignorance.'

---

* Neil Johnson is Head of News and Current Affairs at Vision Christian Media; Host of the weekday program 20Twenty; Author of *Public Christians in a Secular Age* 2022.

1 De Klerk's Question for Whites: 'Do You Support Reform?': South Africa: President unveils wording of referendum that poses a make-or-break test for his government. - Los Angeles Times (latimes.com)

Given that 6 in 10 Aboriginal and Torres Strait Islander people identify as Christian, a defined Christian view should be carefully considered. A 'peacemaker's paradigm' considers a view where the value of people is prioritised. It's how we evaluate what's fair with faith, centred in the biblical Gospel, aligning our identity with Christ, and enabling a view of the world with purpose found in the Divine. In this chapter we look beyond a single moment at a polling booth to the context of what comes in relational hopes and aspirations beyond the referendum.

If the YES vote prevails, political and legal minds will advance their aspirations for Aboriginal and Torres Strait Islander peoples. We have all been weighing the emotive arguments for both sides, and for many Australians we'll try to discern the difference between truth and ideologically driven propaganda.

Since the beginning of our 2023 national debate, I have been conscious to offer an opportunity for developing a Christian view of the emerging arguments.

1. **Essential Racial Equality**

Contrary to a secularised view that divides people by skin tone, the Christian view carries a dynamic that nurtures a foundation for essential racial equality. One might imagine the question put to the Australian people comes in the guise of the now commonly held idea portraying one colour as 'victim' and the other as 'perpetrator' of historic injustice. We might predict what is coming. Earlier generations would be held to account for perceived injustices including expectation of future activist demands for reparations as compensation for past wrongs.

In the debate for an Indigenous Voice to the Parliament, these sentiments are simmering just below the surface of a modest change to the wording in the Australian constitution. There is a necessary caution where a loaded question pre-empts a permanent division of people according to skin colour, historic and cultural heritage. A peacemaker's paradigm resists population division according to perceived racial inequality. The Biblical narrative portrays the intrinsic value of people not based on skin colour but with reference to common ancestry. Not as many races evolved, but as one 'human race' created.[2]

### 2. Disruption to Reconciliation

For the ordinary Australian voter anxious for a unifying outcome the Voice debate is a disruption in the pursuit of reconciliation. It is an unnecessary obstacle to the betterment of relations between Indigenous and non-Indigenous Australians. A peacemaker paradigm wrestles with a true aspiration. Do we pursue those things which unite all Australians as we reflect the context that we are still a young nation? Or do we risk a racially divided future? Common sense in the pursuit of harmony encourages our resistance to those things which may risk entrenched division according to our racial roots whether they be Indigenous, colonial, or migrant.

### 3. Activism or Aspirational Leadership?

As one who sees his role, not as a YES or NO activist, but a minister of the Christian Gospel, I have recognised a little acknowledged dimension to the dynamics of the year-long debate. Whatever the outcome, and whatever the consequences of legislated change, we must not paralyse the pursuit of a movement towards reconciliation. Entrenched division can only be an obstacle to true

2 Genesis 1:27

reconciliation, which is less about the destination and more about the journey together. Those who bear the image of the ultimate Divine 'peacemaker' cannot fail to honour both Aboriginal Australians and non-Aboriginal Australians who advocate for a better future, no matter whether there is a vote for either side of the emotionally charged YES/NO divide.

### 4. Historic Injustice

The Voice to the parliament will trigger a revision of history. Revisionists have been feverishly reworking historic narratives. Realists can never be deaf to claims of displacement and oppression. Yes, there are horrific stories of disadvantage, mistreatment, and historic atrocities by early settlers who displaced tribal culture and lands. The Christian community is not naive to revisionism. In recent years numerous new books have emerged, reflecting the history of Australia with the Christian formation of a nation under rising threat from the 'wokeism' of secular revisionists. Woke secularist revisionism will dismiss colonial and Christian history in the same ways as the current sexual revolution has created its own revision. You might even argue that secular culture dismisses Christian history in the same way that colonial history is accused of dismissing Aboriginal history. Under a YES victory a new 'Truth Telling' history will birth a different narrative of our national history. This dismissal may be a feature addressed by a Peacemaker's Paradigm. Christian dimensions of our national history will be all the more significant. The realities documented by historians including Dr John Harris, and Professor Stuart Piggin show that historic Black and White relations in Church-run 'Missions' that emerged from the early colony, became crucially important in the 1800's. Missions became places of sanctuary and protection for Aboriginal people in the ensuing century beyond the arrival of the First Fleet.

It was Christian mission driven by compassion that offered protection for so many Aboriginal people forced to flee the violence of rogue settlers. In the pursuit of truth-telling we might agree that there has been shameful treatment of fellow human beings as sub-human and relegated to the lowest of status. Christian missionary action has been a glimmer of light and hope, and a demonstration of love and goodwill on a dark landscape. This goodwill between Church and Aboriginal people remains an historic deposit in a bank of goodwill that may be important as we face a difficult future. Missions were motivated by the biblical shaping of value for 'the other,' no matter what skin colour, affirming that all people are 'created in the image and likeness of God.' It is a primary truth with the most practical of applications, that we glean from the opening chapters of Genesis that sets our hierarchical place as one human race, equal before God as creator.

### 5. Missions – More Than Food and Shelter

As the 19th century took hold, amidst the unfolding tensions displacement and mistreatment, an additional dimension of Christian love and equality began to unfold around the biblical view of freedom. Australian Outback Historian Dr Paul Roe identifies the formation of what he calls 'Australia's own Civil Rights Movement.'[3] A prevailing view was that the Aboriginal people were uneducated, and unredeemable. But Christian missionaries began to incubate the formation of leadership for Aboriginal people.

Paul Roe tells the story of a young couple in the 1880's named Daniel and Janet Matthews who formed a Mission school in Echuca. They started Maloga Aboriginal School on the Big Bend of the Murray

3 Dr Paul Roe, Australia's Civil Rights Movement has Christian Roots – 29th Mar 2023 Podcast - https://omny.fm/shows/20twenty/australias-civil-rights-movement-christian-roots-d

River. Daniel recognised the terrible things that were happening to the Aboriginal people. The mission became known as the 'only safe space' in NSW. Daniel would go into the camps where Aboriginal girls were chained to their beds, fighting to free them. Many who found sanctuary in the Mission began to understand the Christian Gospel. A group of students were included in a team to travel to Melbourne to participate in a mission on Brighton beach where the singing and preaching attracted a young Indian man named Thomas Shadrach James[4] who had a Christian background and who was studying to be a doctor but was unable to complete his study due to a tremor in his hand. Daniel asked Thomas to return with him and to teach at the mission school. He agreed, and after working for the first two years without payment, he continued to serve for 40 years. Thomas Shadrach James instructed children by day, and he taught adults at night. Additional to literacy and numeracy, Thomas Shadrach James taught his students to lead, write letters, stand up for themselves, make petitions and put their case affirming that Aboriginal people have a right in Australia to be recognised.

Among his students were the likes of William Cooper[5] who became an Indigenous campaigner advocating for an Aboriginal voice in the parliament and a treaty in the 1930's. Also, so were Sir Douglas Nichols[6] and his wife Gladys. Douglas Nichols was renowned as a great Australian pioneering campaigner for reconciliation. Sir Douglas was eventually appointed Governor of South Australia

4 Australia Day - Our Christian History - Dr Paul Roe (Outback Historian) - 26 Jan 2023 - 20Twenty - Omny.fm Also Biography - Thomas Shadrach James - Australian Dictionary of Biography (anu.edu.au)

5 Dr Paul Roe – the Outback Historian Australia's Civil Rights Movement - Christian Roots - Dr Paul Roe || 20Twenty with Neil Johnson - YouTube Also Biography - William Cooper - Australian Dictionary of Biography (anu.edu.au)

6 Douglas Nichols MBE (1957) and OBE (1968) and knighted (1972). He was named Victorian 'Father of the Year' in 1972. He was Victoria's second Aboriginal justice of the peace, and in 1976 he was appointed Governor of South Australia. Australian Dictionary of Biography - Sir Douglas Ralph (Doug) Nicholls - Australian Dictionary of Biography (anu.edu.au)

(1976). Thomas Shadrach James taught his Aboriginal students that they have a voice, and how to use it. In a broad brushstroke, we might conclude that it was Christian missionaries who were the early champion of reconciliation, and the foundation of a 'voice' for Aboriginal and Torres Strait Islander peoples.

With an ingrained ethic of human racial equality those courageous Christian mission pastors and teachers played a vital role in the protection of Aboriginal people. However, mission endeavours are localised and rarely without shortcomings. Whatever good they achieved, it was not sufficient to hold back the violence well documented, towards Aboriginal people. As leading Historian Dr John Harris[7] the author of the substantial research volume 'One Blood' told me, what the missionaries did was good and noble, but it was never enough.

For many Australians, the necessity to divide goodwill intention with a YES or NO vote is tempered by the important dimension, of searching within ourselves for a deeper way of honouring Aboriginal and Torres Strait Islander peoples, acknowledging their pain, and learning to celebrate their history. The robust debate, or the emotional propaganda wars of the referendum campaign highlights the sensitivities. Australians of goodwill are open to understand the murky turbulence of colonial history. Our prayer might be that every Australian might know by the time of the referendum, the hearts-cry of the Aboriginal people for acknowledgement. As one of the most senior Aboriginal leaders, and founder of The Grasstree Gathering Aunty Jean Phillips[8] shared with me, a YES vote would have a secondary dimension sending a deep and encouraging message to Aboriginal people

7 The book 'One Blood' is a landmark study of two centuries of Aboriginal encounter with Christianity. A resource describing incidents of massacre of Aboriginal people, and the sanctuary many found in mission stations. https://www.chr.org.au/books/ONEBLOOD.pdf

8 Aunty Jean Phillips #BecauseOfHerWeCan | NAIDOC Week | Common Grace

of 'Yes, we are with you.'[9] No matter what the outcome of the referendum, the exercise will be wasted if Australians have failed to hear and recognise the value of Aboriginal and Torres Strait Islander communities.

### 6. Risking Total Loss

Cairns-based Aboriginal Pastors Norman and Barbara Miller echo their deep concerns about what is driving the politics of The Voice. They have not given up hope that the question to the Australian people can change before the vote. They are advocates for a two-tiered question:

1. Recognition of Aboriginal people in the Constitution.
2. And separate legislation for a Voice to the Parliament.

According to the Millers, the present question in its uncertainty and vague detail, risks denying the opportunity for Aboriginal people to win the hearts of Australians for constitutional inclusion. They say an insistence for a constitutional 'Voice to the Parliament' may be the very factor that causes the recognition of Aboriginal and Torres Strait Islander people to be lost.

### 7. One Tribe Australia

A 'peacemaker's paradigm' reflects a dimension that goes beyond the secular driven racial divide. It draws on the transcendent purpose and presence of God in our Australian context. With 6 in 10 Aboriginal people identifying as Christian, there are concerns that the faith dimension of Aboriginal people is being ignored. Our reconciliation journey may be better characterised as a 'One Tribe'

9 See https://player.fm/series/20twenty/the-voice-christian-aboriginal-leaders-aunty-jean-phillips-and-brooke-prentice-16-feb-2023

aspiration, as much as a 'One Family' or 'One Nation,' contrasted to the concepts of material battles for power, ownership, and reparation. The success of the referendum journey will come with a response to the question 'Has the heart-felt concern of Aboriginal and Torres Strait Islander peoples be heard?' 'Will there be a continuation of recognition that inalienable rights under the law, are to be shared by all skin colours, no matter the outcome of the referendum?' It should be no surprise that the image of Christ who suffered the brutality of 'The Cross' is the most unifying symbol for those who feel alienation and rejection or the brutality of oppression. The Christian symbol of hope cuts across every divide, humbling hearts before one transcendent God.

By now, undecided voters on the referendum question will be leaning one way or another. Many voters will be swayed, depending on the media they listen to. The cultural echo chambers aligning to the left or the right, are hammering home ideological positions, keeping their sides engaged.

For those with goodwill towards Aboriginal and Torres Strait Islanders, many have waited as the debate matures to take a position of wisdom, not one of ignorance. Understanding arguments, by honouring, and appreciating what is at risk is the least effort required if we are to settle on a position that produces a better future.

If a YES vote is successful, there will be the further pursuit of the direction outlined in the Uluru Statement from The Heart, that proposes more dimensions: A Voice to the Parliament, then Treaty, and Truth-telling.

I encourage a view of the referendum that takes us beyond a mark on the ballot paper. A view that maintains a constitutional equality before the law. It's a view of reconciliation that embraces a Divinely appointed dimension and encourages the Christian community that our journey alongside Aboriginal people is not over. 'Blessed are the peacemakers for they will be called children of God.' (Matt 5:9 NIV)

# 7

# WHAT THE GOOD SAMARITAN TEACHES US ABOUT THE VOICE TO PARLIAMENT

**Julie Sladden***

In 2022 I read the Australian Constitution for the very first time. I would like to say that I did this of my own accord, but I didn't. It was a course requirement. If it weren't for that, I probably would have happily continued my life, as a medical doctor, not having never read it. I'm glad I now have.

The self-described 'birth certificate of a nation' sets out the basic rules for our system of Government. It was surprising how much I intuitively knew. But much was also demystified regarding the structure and function of the Australian Government. Taking over ten years to conceive, debate, write and approve, it's clear much care and attention was given to the process of writing Australia's Constitution.

In a recent interview, Nicholas Aroney, who is professor of constitutional law at the University of Queensland, outlined just how much care was given to this process. Professor Aroney stated:

> *The framers of the Constitution when they were deliberating about it in the 1890s, read all of the books that were there to*

* Julie Sladden is a medical doctor, founding director of Australians for Science and Freedom, and Local Government Councillor for the West Tamar in Tasmania.

*be read, at least in the English-speaking world, on what good governance looks like and what good constitutions look like. And they looked really closely at the way other constitutions operate in other countries - the United States, Canada, the United Kingdom. They also had all of their experiences at a colonial level because they were representatives of the six self-governing colonies in Australia and so they had a lot of experience of what it meant to have constitutional government and representative democracy. And they brought all of this learning into the process of constitution making."*[1]

Passed in 1900 as part of a British Act of Parliament, and taking effect on 1 January 1901, the Australian Constitution behaves not unlike a computer operating system that provides the framework and rules for a user to perform a desired task. If all is working well, the user is rarely thinking about the operating system they are using. Instead, they have the freedom to think about the task. In the same way, a well-functioning constitution allows the smooth operation of government to occur so that the people can perform the 'tasks' of living in community.

### 1. Three distinct characteristics I admire about Australia's Constitution

Firstly, the Constitution divides political power. History has shown time and again what concentrated and centralised power does to governments and the people. Professor Aroney explains:

*One of the South Australian delegates expressed concern that over-centralization creates a vortex into which power gets concentrated. And when that happens, people lose liberty because the government becomes very distant from them. And once it becomes distant and become centralized and concentrated, the capacity of the people to influence the*

1 John Anderson and Nicholas Aroney, 'The Voice and the Constitution', 17 March 2023, at https://youtu.be/cs4TMsSQnOI.

> *government and even resist when it's overreaching, becomes weaker. The federal system is really important in our system because it diversifies power.*[2]

Secondly, the Constitution is deliberately blind to gender, wealth, religion, and race. All Australians are considered equal. An appreciation of the past 200 years of Australian history shows this equality has taken a while to manifest and is indeed still manifesting. Although the Commonwealth Electoral Act 1962 gave all Aboriginal and Torres Strait Islander people the option to vote, it was not until the Commonwealth Electoral Amendment Act 1983 that made enrolling to vote at federal elections compulsory. In this way, the Constitution guides the people toward the foundational principle of equality for all Australians.

The final characteristic of the Constitution are the precise requirements for change in this document to be enacted. It seems the writers made this deliberately hard. Not to make the people stumble, but in recognition of human nature: that we are susceptible to influences of power, money, and corruption. It is important that democracy be protected from those in positions of power or influence who might use constitutional change for their advantage. Any constitutional change should be a true desire of the people of that democracy. The writers of our Constitution thought long and hard about what should be included. In the same way, Australians must think long and hard before any change is enacted that might affect the generations that follow.

The proposed 'Voice to Parliament' has given Australians the opportunity to consider whether it is time to change the Constitution. In light of the above explanation, it's important that we, the current generation, take on the responsibility of seriously considering the potential consequences of such a change.

2 Ibid.

I recently had the opportunity to meet with local elected members from around Australia and found myself sharing a lunchtime discussion with a fellow Councillor from the Northern Territory. After covering the usual 'rates, roads and rubbish' waypoints, I asked my colleague if they would mind sharing their views on the proposed constitutional changes.

"I'm all for it," he said. "I was born shortly after we got the right to vote and The Voice is something I am very passionate about." As I listened it was clear this Councillor was concerned for his community and committed to ensuring better outcomes for the people he represented. Our discussion covered health, roads, housing, education and future opportunities and on all facets we were aligned. Our common ground was that we both wanted better outcomes for Aboriginal Australians. Our differences lay in how this might be achieved and it is from this perspective that questions and concerns about the proposed Voice have formed in my mind.

## 2. Questions and concerns

How can we know that a 'top-down' centralised governmental approach, will result in the grassroots positive effects that we are hoping to see?

Consider the principle of subsidiarity: that social and political issues are best dealt with at the most local level the issue can be successfully resolved. Accordingly, 'the principle is premised upon empowering the citizen, with decision-making carried out as close to the citizen as is viable'.[3] Following this principle means the federal government should only do what the state can't, and the state government should only do what local government

3 See: Michelle Evans and Augusto Zimmermann, 'The Global Reference of Subsidiarity', in M. Evans and A. Zimmermann (eds.), *Global Perspectives on Subsidiarity* (Springer, 2014) 1.

can't, and local government should only do what individuals and communities can't. "When things are done at a local level, people can engage in their own self-government. And when people engage in their own self-government, they usually do it better," says Professor Aroney.

How will over 600 nations of diverse opinions, views and needs be consolidated into one Voice to Parliament? The proposed changes have divided the nation and there is a distinct lack of consensus from Aboriginal communities with a number of high-profile Aboriginal Australians indicating they do not support 'The Voice.' With, often small, local areas including up to three or four distinct nations, how would a local 'voice' be able to adequately represent the people when there is such a diversity of views and needs? Following on from that, how do we avoid the 'Voice' becoming hijacked by the noisy, or powerful few?

A number of mechanisms – including legislation and practical policy making – already exist to address the problems we are seeing manifest in the community. If these mechanisms aren't working, *why* aren't they working?

Does a call for the Voice imply that elected representatives are not doing their job? Australia currently has eleven Aboriginal members in federal parliament, equating to 4.9 per cent representation for 3.2 per cent of the population who identifies as Aboriginal or Torres Strait Islander. In addition, there is a federal minister for Indigenous Australians and a minister for Aboriginal affairs in each state and territory. Aboriginal Australians have a number of voices in parliament already, if their voices aren't being heard, then why?

My final and gravest concern is how can a change to the Constitution which divides the nation based on race, possibly pave the way to healing and unity in this country? For Aboriginal Elder Kerry White, it won't. "A bit over two hundred years ago", she says,

> *they rounded Aboriginal people up and locked them on missions. So Aboriginal people were segregated from White society. Then we come forward to now – 'The Voice' – and they're segregating up again. They're taking us back two hundred years… it's back to segregation. And frankly, it's racist towards our White brothers and sisters that live in this land with us.*[4]

### 3. The conversation that's not happening

There seems to be a distinct lack of open debate and discussion about the issues, potential challenges, pitfalls, costs, and benefits. Moreover, there seems to be a distinct lack of diversity of views reported in the media. I have listened to presentations, speeches, and interviews, and read countless articles for the 'Yes' vote. None of which have offered more than – dare I say it – high level virtue signalling. The real discussion seems to be happening over on the other side.

From the federal government there is a distinct lack of specific detail on how the Voice would function on a local, state. and federal level. Despite this, the public messaging in the media is strong, and several sporting codes and high-profile companies have proudly endorsed 'The Voice' encouraging supporters to do likewise.

The lack of open debate and detail, and public messaging have inevitably led to an unbalanced conversation and a nation deprived of awareness and understanding. This seems to extend back beyond the Uluru Statement, which calls for the establishment of a First Nations Voice and a Makaratta Commission – or treaty between Indigenous and non-indigenous Australians. The statement, signed by 250 delegates, is being used as a consensus statement for the Voice. However, it was recently reported that some of these signatories had not been made aware what they were signing, and how the statement would be used.[5]

---

4 Steven Tripp, 'What I learned from an Aboriginal Elder', *The Spectator Australia*, 13 December 2022, at https://www.spectator.com.au/2022/12/what-i-learnt-from-an-aboriginal-elder/.

5 Sarah Ison, 'Uluru statement signatories "surprised"', *The Weekend Australian*, 17-

## 4. The Good Samaritan teaches us a lesson or two

Here is where I can't help being reminded of the story of the 'good Samaritan', a parable Jesus used to eloquently demonstrate what it means to 'love your neighbour.' You can read it in Luke 10: 25-37. To my mind there are two important lessons in this story. Firstly, of the three potential helpers for the injured man – the priest, the Levite, and the Samaritan – the Samaritan was assumed, culturally, to be least likely to help. Despite these expectations the Samaritan did everything he could to provide for the need of the injured stranger. He ignored the divisions of the day and simply got on with helping his neighbour.

The second lesson is this, no amount of government intervention can beat individuals and communities taking responsibility at a local level. I'm pretty sure if the Samaritan had instead, continued on his way, reported the robbery, and waited for the authorities to respond, the outcome would have been quite different.

This brings me to my final point; the Constitution is only as effective as the culture it serves.[6] As Professor Aroney explains:

> *You can have the finest constitution in the world with all of the right words in it, but it's the people operating under it. If the political culture in which it operates, doesn't have respect for the rule of law, doesn't have respect for following proper procedures, then people will manipulate the document to achieve their own ends.*[7]

We should be focussing on changing the culture, not the Constitution, striving for a culture that promotes unity, not

18 June 2023.

6 See: Augusto Zimmermann, 'The Rule of Law as a Culture of Legality: Legal and Extra-legal Elements for the Realisation of the Rule of Law in Society' (2007) 15 *Murdoch University Journal of Law* 10, 24-28.

7 John Anderson and Nicholas Aroney, 'The Voice and the Constitution', 17 March 2023, at https://youtu.be/cs4TMsSQnOI.

division; healing not hypocrisy; respectful debate not stifling free speech. We should be taking responsibility at all levels of the community, including ourselves. And, ultimately, loving our neighbour, like the good Samaritan did.

# 8
# A RETURN TO SEGREGATION

**Thomas Eglinton***

We are raised on horror stories of racial segregation. Who has not seen pictures of the signs: "No Blacks Allowed"? Who has not seen the buses with a black section and a white section?

We instinctively know that this sort of segregation is wrong because it is divisive. It divides, even destroys, communities, and it breeds wars.

I thought that we had moved on. I thought that we had rejected segregation. Until I heard about *The Indigenous Voice to Parliament*, which returns Australia to a state of segregation.

## 1. Are Aboriginal Australians Disadvantaged?

*The Voice* is based on the idea that Indigenous Australians are not real Australians.

I can partially understand where the authors of the *Uluru Statement from the Heart* (the 2017 document that demands a Voice to Parliament) are coming from. History often contains grievous things, and the history of Australia is no exception. Take, for instance, this statement from Sir Edward Barton, the first Prime Minister of Australia, made on 26 September 1901:

---

* Thomas Eglinton is a Pastor at Smithfield Baptist Church. Founded in 1846, Smithfield Baptist Church is a Reformed *Baptist church* located in Sydney's South West.

> *I do not think either that the doctrine of the equality of man was really ever intended to include racial equality. There is no racial equality. There is that basic inequality. These races are in comparison with white races – I think no one wants convincing of this fact – unequal and inferior.*[1]

Barton was not talking about Indigenous Australians (he was discussing Immigration Policy) and he wished no harm upon those races he viewed to be 'inferior', but this view does display racism.

From the founding of Australia, Indigenous Australians were excluded from the Australian Constitution and from the Census; they were not always given a vote and were, at times, treated as non-existent. The naming of Australia as *Terra Nullius* or 'nobody's land' is a demonstration of how the colonisers viewed the Indigenous peoples.

Naturally, history is full of terrible things and these aspects of Australia's history are bad. But there are many good things in our history as well. Some of those good things have happened in relation to Indigenous Australians.

In 1962, Indigenous Australians were given the right to vote in Australian Federal Elections. In the 1850s Aboriginal men could vote in Victoria, New South Wales, and South Australia but it took until 1965 for all states to grant this right. The Constitution was changed in 1967 to ensure the recognition of Indigenous people as citizens of Australia. From that point on, the Parliament was not excluded from making laws regarding Indigenous people. In 1988 and 1992, the High Court, in its *Mabo* decisions, recognised that Australia was not *terra nullius*.[2]

1 Edmund Barton, 'Immigration Restriction Bill', House of Representatives, Debates, 26 September 1901, 5233

2 *Mabo v Queensland (No 1)* (1988) 166 CLR 186.; *Mabo and Others v. Queensland (No. 2)* (1992) 175 CLR 1

In 2023, Indigenous Australians are not excluded from our Constitution. They are included in exactly the same way as every other Australian.

Indigenous Australians are represented in Parliament. They are not excluded from voting or lobbying Parliament.

And they are not excluded from being recognised as living in Australia before European settlers arrived. In fact, you can hardly go a day in today's Australia without being reminded of that very fact through the ubiquitous 'Welcome to Country' and 'Acknowledgement of Country' announcements.

Aboriginal people are recognised everywhere, and Indigenous people and other Australians are treated equally.

2023 is not 1901.

### 2. The Voice is Segregation

So, why would we go backwards? Why would we move to a situation where we are once again segregating Indigenous Australians and making them something other than Australians? Why would we create a whole sub-group of Australians and mark them out as something different to the rest of us?

The promoters of *The Voice to Parliament* clearly articulate that segregation is precisely what they are after. In a video on the training platform on the *Uluru Statement from the Heart* website, Dean Parker (Director, From the Heart), says that their goal is to have "a unique status as the first peoples of the Australian nation."

This immediately segregates Indigenous Australians. But that is not the end. Parker goes on to say that "we can't just have symbolic recognition."

This is not just about stating that there were people here before

European settlement. More is being demanded. Eddie Synot (Uluru Dialogue, UNSW) puts it this way, "Not only are you recognising us, finally, but you actually have to listen to us and talk to us, and we have a say, we get to sit at the table where the decisions are made which for too long have been made without us."[3]

The goal of *The Voice to Parliament* is therefore to have Indigenous Australians set apart as different to all other Australians. This is a return to the divided and crumbling societies of times past.

This is segregation.

### 3. Positive Segregation is Still Segregation

It could be argued that something like *The Voice* is positive segregation. It advantages a particular group based on their race, rather than disadvantaging a group. Someone might say that *The Voice* is different from not allowing Black Americans into the Whites' bathroom and requiring them to use a 'Black-only' bathroom that is not as good.

There are two problems with this argument.

The first problem is the definition of racism.

According to the Australian Human Rights Commission, racism is "the process by which systems and policies, actions and attitudes create inequitable opportunities and outcomes for people based on race. Racism is more than just prejudice in thought or action. It occurs when this prejudice – whether individual or institutional – is accompanied by the power to discriminate against, oppress or

3 The Uluru Statement from the Heart training videos, accessed March 2023 (https://ulurustatement.org/training/#/)

limit the rights of others."[4]

The Human Rights Commission continues: "Racism includes all the laws, policies, ideologies and barriers that prevent people from experiencing justice, dignity, and equity because of their racial identity."

As can be seen, racism is about laws that create inequality based on racial identity. Racism is creating systems that have the power to limit the rights of others.

If there is a bathroom that only people from a certain race are allowed to use, then that system is racist because it is designed to differentiate between citizens based on their race, which is an involuntary characteristic. It does not matter if it is a special bathroom with special privileges and special trappings – gold taps, marble tiles, silk hand towels and fully-recycled 4-ply toilet paper!

The second problem is that having one privileged race requires that all the other races not have the same privilege. Positive segregation towards one race involves negative segregation towards all the others. Hence, if you are not Indigenous you will not be allowed to participate in *The Voice to Parliament*. This will mean that you will have your rights limited. You will not have the same access to the leaders of our country as Aboriginal citizens.

The Voice is positive segregation and positive segregation is still racist. Indigenous Australians are already full and free Australian citizens. Like all Australians, they have full recognition in the courts, and they have a voice to parliament through their vote and through the ability to consult with and petition parliament.

Our political system is not perfect, and it can be modified over time.

---

4 'What is Racism?', Australian Human Rights Commission, at https://humanrights.gov.au/our-work/race-discrimination/what-racism, accessed 24 April 2023.

But *The Voice* proposal basically enshrines racism and division in the Australian Constitution, the most important document of our land. At the moment, the Constitution is not racist because every Australian is presented as equal. This is how it should be. If there is racism elsewhere, then it needs to be dealt with elsewhere. But the Constitution is not the problem and is not the place to entrench a divisive solution like *The Voice to Parliament*.

### 4. Racism is Unbiblical

Racism feels wrong to us today. The Australian Human Rights Commission thinks that racism is wrong. But what does the Bible have to say?

Race is defined by the Merriam-Webster dictionary as 'any one of the groups that humans are often divided into based on physical traits regarded as common among people of shared ancestry.'

That is, race is defined by your ancestors and your appearance.

If this is the definition, then according to the Bible there is only one race. We all come from the same parents, and we all look the same. In Genesis chapter 1-2, God made our first parents – Adam and Eve.

> *And Adam called his wife's name Eve, because she was the mother of all living (Genesis 3:20, NKJV).*

The Bible teaches that every person who has ever lived can trace their ancestry back to Adam and Eve. We all share a family resemblance because of this. Even physically, all humans share significant common features. This is built-in to creation.

> *And Adam lived one hundred and thirty years, and begot a son* ***in his own likeness****, after his image, and named him Seth (Genesis 5:3, NKJV).*

Racism is unbiblical because race (as defined above) is a man-made construct. People are never treated as more or less valuable in the Bible based on their physical appearance and their ancestry. This is why Christians should strongly reject this proposal to divide our nation based on ancestry and appearance.

### 5. Culture and Nationhood are Different to Race

You might be wondering about how there can be no concept of race in the Bible when there is clearly a concept of different groups of people.

> *After these things I looked, and behold, a great multitude … of all nations, tribes, peoples, and tongues, standing before the throne and before the Lamb … saying, 'Salvation belongs to our God who sits on the throne, and to the Lamb!'* [5]

God does recognise that people form groups and that these groups can be defined. There are distinct nations in the world. There are tribes of people, and you can draw a circle around them.

I suggest that a helpful (though not comprehensive) concept to help in defining these groups is the idea of culture. According to the *Encyclopedia Britannica,* culture 'includes language, ideas, beliefs, customs, codes, institutions, tools, techniques, works of art, rituals, and ceremonies, among other elements.' Culture is the particular characteristics of a people group. Importantly, culture includes 'beliefs' as well as 'codes' or 'values'.

As our Australian society seeks to be multi-cultural, we need to be aware that not all cultural elements are spiritually neutral. Some aspects of culture seem neutral – such as food, clothing, or language. But even in these elements we can quickly see that

5 Revelation 7:8-9, NKJV.

spirituality is lurking.

> *The things which the Gentiles sacrifice they sacrifice to demons and not to God, and I do not want you to have fellowship with demons. You cannot drink the cup of the Lord and the cup of demons; you cannot partake of the Lord's table and of the table of demons."*[6]

The Apostle Paul explicitly tells the Corinthian Christians to watch what they eat because sometimes eating at the cultural food festivals means fellowshipping with demons. All people groups have spirituality interwoven throughout their cultures. Some of this spirituality is good – when it is worshipping the Triune God of the Bible. Some must be rejected by Christians – when it is worshipping idols.

The Bible teaches that Jesus has come to redeem a people *out of* every tribe, tongue, and nation. That being so, those who follow Him will reject the idol worship ingrained in their culture and start to cry out in worship to God and His Son Jesus Christ.

### 6. Paganism and The Uluru Statement from the Heart

The *Uluru Statement from the Heart* is a pagan document. It explicitly articulates nature worship and ancestor worship. The writers speak of Aboriginal sovereignty which 'is a spiritual notion: the ancestral tie between the land, or 'mother nature', and the Aboriginal and Torres Strait Islander peoples who were born therefrom, remain attached thereto, and must one day return thither to be united with our ancestors.'

It is this spiritual bond that the writers say gives them claim on the land. This spirituality forms an integral part of the culture that

6 1 Corinthians 10:20-21, NKJV.

'will be a gift to [Australia].'

Christians must have their eyes wide open to the spirituality that is interwoven throughout Aboriginal culture. Those who are behind the *Uluru Statement from the Heart* have clearly stated that they want to influence Australian society through *The Voice to Parliament*. They have said that one purpose of *The Voice* is to 'empower' Indigenous people to gift their culture to Australia. The culture they are speaking of is born out of the worship of nature and ancestors.

My fellow Australians, we must think carefully about a change to the foundational way that our nation works. Do we really want to enshrine race-based divisions in our Constitution? Do we want to return to racial segregation? And have we understood the spiritual elements that are at work, underlying the proposal of *The Uluru Statement from the Heart* and *The Voice to Parliament*?

# 9

# THE VOICE AND FREEDOM OF RELIGION

**Dave Pellowe**[*]

I believe in the separation of Church and State. It is a principle as essential to a healthy democracy as are its sisters: a free and independent press, freedom of speech, and the rights to peaceful assembly and protest.

There is a common confusion of the meaning and origins of the principle behind that phrase, but it is most easily understood by its context, located in the First Amendment to the Constitution of the United States of America.

The precise phrase "separation of Church and State" is not found in any constitution or legislation there or here in Australi a. It was first coined and therefore defined by one of the framers of the United States Constitution, Thomas Jefferson – probably the least religious of all its Founding Fathers.

He was responding to concerns about eroding religious liberty raised by the Danbury Baptist Association in Connecticut. Jefferson agreed religion was something the government must never interfere in. However, his letter, and the famous phrase

[*] Dave Pellowe is the director of Church And State Ministries, convening the annual Australian Church And State Summit and various conferences around Australia throughout each year, and presenter of The Church And State Show, produced by The Good Sauce and which airs weekly on ADH.TV.

he coined therein, can in no way be construed as asserting that religion must never interfere with public policy or government services. [1]

The Supreme Court of the United States has often misinterpreted the meaning of the phrase "separation of Church and State". This is a consequence of activist justices making decisions according to their preferred outcomes, instead of adhering faithfully to the original intents of the words written in the Constitution.

Thomas Jefferson directly referred to the religious clause of the First Amendment as "a wall of separation between Church and State." In the context of eliminating the government's power to make laws curbing the freedom of speech, the freedom of the press, the freedom of peaceful assembly and the freedom of protest, it is irrational to infer the mention of religion was intended to expand the power of government, and not to also free the people to choose any religion they preferred.

By proximity to those other clauses in the First Amendment, as well as the historical context of framers who opposed government excesses and tyranny more than anything else, "separation of Church and State" can easily be understood to instead be a check and balance on the government, along with the other freedoms used to scrutinise and criticise government decisions.

The Prime Minister, Anthony Albanese, is on a crash course to tear down that "wall of separation" between religion and government and to violate our own, equivalent clause found in Section 116 of the Australian Constitution.

Twelve seconds into his victory speech on the night he was elected to become the 31st Prime Minister of Australia, Anthony Albanese spoke eleven words that ominously promised to divide and

---

1 'Jefferson Letter to the Danbury Baptists', January 1, 1802, at https://www.loc.gov/loc/lcib/9806/danpre.html.

damage a nation pursuing racial harmony and religious liberalism (if not secularism).

Either he was blissfully ignorant of the reasonably foreseeable collateral damage the debate alone would cause, or cavalierly indifferent, in the pursuit of the intoxicating opportunity to impose his vision of society.

Just eleven words described a three-part manifesto to dilute the political power of the average voter and to thrust a political spear through the thigh of our nation ("Makarrata"). Albanese's simple words heralded a coming campaign to add a whole new chapter to the Constitution (the "Voice"), to hand extraordinary new powers to an activist class including too many jurists (treaty), and to rewrite Australian history to suit the rent seekers of the Racial Grievance Industry ("truth" telling).

These eleven beguiling words reveal that the Prime Minister's agenda is every bit as radical as that of Senator Lidia Thorpe:

*"I commit to the Uluru Statement from The Heart in Full".*

The Australian people did vote for a change from the uninspiring previous Government, even if they didn't fully understand what they would get instead. Now we're being asked to vote for change again this year: a permanent change to one of the ten oldest, most stable and successful national constitutions in the world.

Our founding fathers naturally built upon the centuries of British jurisprudence we inherited and carefully studied the grand American experiment in democracy, and crafted our own, exceptional constitution. Like the United States, one of the obviously deliberate designs foundational to our national political stability and enduring peace is that of forbidding the Commonwealth to establish or impose any religion, or to require any religious conformity of a person holding any Commonwealth position.

Section 116 of the Australian Constitution stipulates, "The Commonwealth shall not make any law for establishing any religion, or for imposing any religious observance, or for prohibiting the free exercise of any religion, and no religious test shall be required as a qualification for any office or public trust under the Commonwealth."

Yet establishing, imposing and requiring Aboriginal religion is fairly obviously what the Prime Minister is proposing by committing "to the Uluru Statement from The Heart in Full."

It is important to note, beyond a commonsense approach to the question of what constitutes religion, that in regard to matters pertaining to the Constitution, Australia's High Court has been generous and inclusive in defining religion. There's not really a strict set of criteria for answering the question about something inherently intangible.

A religion does not have to be formalised or organised in the sense Westerners are accustomed to in order to be recognised as a religion. Such a limited view of what constitutes a religion would be the kind of Western cultural imperialism which illiberal progressives would normally object to (when convenient).

It is reasonable to instead look for a quantity of elements or features comparable to other recognised religions, even if there are differences in the weight given to them or the ways they are observed by various participants in that religion. Some basic questions one could ask about a belief system to honestly conclude whether it constitutes a religion are:

1. Is there a basic belief in a realm of existence other than but just as real as the physical, usually (but not necessarily) spiritual or supernatural?

2. Is there a belief that the nature of people is more than physical, but also something like a spirit?
3. Is there a belief about the eternal destiny of people after death, either physical or spiritual?
4. Is there a belief about the origins of everything that exists, especially supernatural or mythical?
5. Is there a belief in a supernatural being or thing (including the universe itself, or parts thereof), not limited to Almighty God or a god?
6. Do adherents themselves view their own set of shared beliefs as constituting religion?

Other elements of most formal or informal religions may include liturgy, ritual/ceremony, dogma, tradition, worship, prayer, sacred objects such as relics and icons, taboos, and inculcation of spiritual beliefs in children and/or converts.

Before we even look at the Uluru Statement from the Heart, let's compare the religious features of common Aboriginal beliefs to the lists above.

Many Aboriginals believe that people have a spirit, and each spirit comes from the land into every baby born there. After death, their spirit returns to the land (believed to be a living entity, called "Country"). Many Aboriginals believe they are therefore spiritually tied to "Country".

These beliefs undergird commonly performed smoking rituals and "Welcome to Country" liturgies to communicate with the spirits of ancestors that the visitor is a friend and to let them travel without harm or interference, as well as to ward off evil spirits.

As a practicing Christian who clearly understands the spiritual meaning and significance of such rituals, I politely excuse myself from them, not wanting to even be possibly confused as a willing participant – just like The Greens do for the Lord's Prayer.

That's fine and that's the liberty we should all protect, and no offense should be intended or taken. Unlike the Greens, I'm not proposing we legislate against others from freely exercising their religion. I'm proposing it is illiberal and regressive to legislate either way.

Further evidence of Aboriginal beliefs constituting a religion are well known to everyone in Aboriginal Creation myths, referred to as "The Dreaming", or "Dream Time" – a period of mythical entities shaping the land and its features which generations have known without significant change.

But whatever insincere debate there may be about the above facts, the Uluru Statement from the Heart must be recognised as a religious as well as a political manifesto. Note the typically religious words like "Creation", "spiritual" and "sacred", and religious ideas of supernatural origins and destinations before and after this life, as well as articulated beliefs in spiritual ties to the land.

> *Our Aboriginal and Torres Strait Islander tribes were the first sovereign Nations of the Australian continent and its adjacent islands, and possessed it under our own laws and customs. This our ancestors did, according to the reckoning of our culture, from the Creation, according to the common law from 'time immemorial', and according to science more than 60,000 years ago.*
>
> *This sovereignty is a spiritual notion: the ancestral tie between the land, or 'mother nature', and the Aboriginal and Torres Strait Islander peoples who were born therefrom, remain attached thereto, and must one day return thither to be united with our ancestors. This link is the basis of the ownership of the soil, or better, of sovereignty. It has never been ceded*

> *or extinguished, and co-exists with the sovereignty of the Crown.*
>
> *How could it be otherwise? That peoples possessed a land for sixty millennia and this sacred link disappears from world history in merely the last two hundred years?"*[2]

It is a clearly religious text, laden with pagan beliefs like animism and ancestor worship. It literally describes Aboriginal sovereignty over this continent as a spiritual and sacred notion: the land as an entity they are born from, remain attached to and return to upon their death. The text signed by so many invited conference delegates agrees this religious belief is <u>the</u> basis of Aboriginal ownership of the land.

In promising to implement this manifesto "in full" as Prime Minister Albanese did, I believe this government violates Section 116 of the Constitution which prohibits the Commonwealth making any law to establish any religion, or to impose any religious observance.

Imposition of Aboriginal religion upon Australians of all religions (or none) by government is something we have unfortunately come to expect. I believe a plurality of Australians are exhausted by the endless Aboriginal rituals at the beginning of every sports match, video meeting and Qantas landing, and are familiar with the scenes of Aboriginal religionists supposedly cleansing an area of evil spirits with smoke, but that is far from the full extent of demolition happening to the wall separating Church and State.

More and more significant, natural Australian landmarks and national parks are being closed to Australians in the name of observing Aboriginal beliefs about sacred rocks and places. Uluru,

2 'Final Report of the Referendum Council', *Referendum Council*, 30 June 2017, at https://www.referendumcouncil.org.au/final-report.html#toc-anchor-ulurustatement-from-the-heart.

the world's largest monolith, was in no danger of erosion or damage from non-indigenous visitors on designated paths under the supervision of rangers – but now Aboriginal religion demands it be called sacred by everyone.

That isn't just a benign, democratic exercise in private property rights as enjoyed by every mosque, synagogue, temple and cathedral. It's an exclusion from public land common to all Australians, by the imposition of one favoured religion upon everyone. Only subjective religious belief as described by the Uluru Statement supports a view which is contrary to public ownership. Mt Warning in northern New South Wales, the Grampians in Victoria and the peaks in Queensland's Glasshouse Mountains are also being asserted as "sacred" to Aboriginal people.

And it's totally fine for them to believe that.

But it violates the principle of the separation of Church and State – of government not establishing a State religion – to legislate that, or to impose that religious observance on anyone let alone everyone.

Yet, it is precisely that religious belief which the drafters of the Uluru Statement from the Heart, and which the Albanese Government has pledged to implement in full that is the foundation for the proposed permanent changes to our Constitution.

Let me move now to the actual proposed design and function of the indigenous "Voice" to Parliament. The 24 Indigenous people appointed to make representations and provide advice will be taxpayer funded public servants of the Commonwealth of Australia.

Will it be possible for anyone who rejects the religious claims of the Uluru Statement, for example a Christian who refuses to endorse pagan beliefs of spiritism and animism, to be appointed to that role? Wouldn't they at a minimum be required to subscribe to the Uluru Statement from the Heart "in full" as the Prime Minister said?

But our Constitution has always said that "No religious test shall be required as a qualification for any office or public trust under the Commonwealth." It seems highly unlikely there won't be at least an informal requirement of some Aboriginal religious belief in prospective members, in clear violation of Section 116.

Are Australians fully aware and accepting that they are being asked to literally enshrine an Aboriginal religion with a new chapter being added to the Constitution? Even if popularly subscribing to that arguably false and pagan religion, are they happy to junk the democratic principle of separation of Church and State to impose their beliefs on everyone else?

It would be one thing if the basis of claim for change was purely historical, or political – but it is neither. If we are to take people at their word, as sincere and honest, then the sole claim for Aboriginal "sovereignty" is *spiritual* – religious.

There is not only one way to close the gap in expected outcomes or to advance reconciliation. There is certainly a better way than the proposed repetition of past failures in bureaucracy with the added snares of permanency and undoing the good work of the 1967 referendum.

I share objectives of peace and prosperity for my fellow Australians in remote communities with those who will be voting "yes" in the referendum, but I remain convinced there are many unresolvable problems with the proposed "Voice" to Parliament. My colleagues contributing to this important book have clearly described and listed many if not most of them in other chapters, and this is but one more.

If the reader believes as I do in the separation of Church and State and Section 116 of the Australian Constitution – that government at any level should never establish a religion, should never impose religious observances on anyone, and should never require certain religious beliefs of public servants – then such readers can only reject the Prime Minister's agenda to implement the religious manifesto called the Uluru Statement from the Heart in full, or any part of it.

# 10

# JOHN PAUL II WOULD NOT HAVE SUPPORTED THE VOICE

**Rocco Loiacono***

Following the election of the Albanese government last year, religious leaders from various Christian denominations and other faiths expressed their support for the proposal to amend the Constitution to include a provision for the Indigenous Voice to Parliament and the Executive. In the church I belong to, the Catholic Church, the Archbishop of Perth, Timothy Costelloe, who is the President of the Australian Catholic Bishops Conference, and the Archbishop of Melbourne, Peter Comensoli, have been particularly fulsome in such support.

Following a meeting in May of this year, the Catholic Bishops' Conference reiterated that support, stating that the Voice "could be a significant step towards a more just and equitable Australia".[1]

---

* Rocco Loiacono is a Senior Lecturer in Law, Curtin University, and is a translator from Italian to English. His work on translation, linguistics, and law has been widely published in peer-reviewed journals.

1 Rosie Lewis, Australia's bishops say Indigenous voice to parliament 'could be a significant step towards a more just and equitable Australia', *The Australian*, 17 May 2023, at https://www.theaustralian.com.au/nation/politics/catholics-promote-uluru-statement-ahead-of-indigenous-voice-to-parliament-referendum/news-story/5f786538ff4fffba2da3fa6be08adadb.

This statement purports to represent a uniform view of the Bishops of Australia on the question.

However, I have been told by one bishop (who for obvious reasons I cannot name) that the view among his fellow prelates on the Voice is not unanimous. As he pointed out: "Whenever the Church marries the spirit of the age, she will be a widow in the next."

I would warn religious leaders to be cautious in their enthusiasm for the Voice.

Just like the declarations of support for the Voice from large corporate organisations and sporting bodies, the declaration of support from the Catholic Bishops' Conference, beyond the obvious 'feel good factor' in the minds of those making such declarations, must be taken with a grain of salt, for several reasons.

First, this is yet another example of bishops preferring politics as opposed to the pastoral concern for their flock. The Voice will actually undermine (for reasons I explain below) the fundamental Christian principle of the inherent dignity of each person, as exemplified in the principle of equality before the law.

The Australian Catholic Bishops' Conference endorsed the Uluru Statement from the Heart in 2021, and in the statement mentioned above said the Constitution's lack of reference to Indigenous people having custodianship of the land was "an omission which needs to be rectified".[2]

"A voice to parliament isn't the only way to achieve that outcome … but it is the way requested by those who gathered at the historic meeting at Uluru," the bishops' statement reads.

"This could be a significant step towards a more just and equitable Australia. We want to encourage all Australians to educate

2 Ibid.

themselves as well as possible concerning the proposal to establish the voice.

"This is an important moment in the history of the nation, and it can help us to move towards a deep and just reconciliation. It also offers a mechanism to improve the lives of Aboriginal and Torres Strait Islander peoples."

They encouraged Catholic parishes, schools, and agencies to "arrange opportunities for people to read the document (Uluru Statement from the Heart) and have discussions about their response to its key messages".

Such a statement belies the fact that the Voice amendment is far more than recognition of Aboriginal people in the Constitution.

If enacted, the Voice would allow some people, based on their race, to have two methods of influencing public policy: through their representatives in parliament and their representatives on the Voice. Such additional influence would not be limited to Indigenous affairs. As stated in the Calma-Langton report:

> *The National Voice would advise on matters of national significance to Aboriginal and Torres Strait Islander peoples … This cannot be restricted to Aboriginal and Torres Strait Islander–specific portfolios, policies and programs, but must also include mainstream services and funding.*
>
> *In other words, the Voice could have a say on everything, and at this point we do not know – or are not being told – what will and what won't be within its scope.*

What is more, Megan Davis, a key Voice proponent, has admitted the Voice will be a first step, followed by a treaty and then "truth-telling".[3]

3 The University of Queensland, Voice, treaty, truth. Q&A with Professor Megan Davis, at https://stories.uq.edu.au/contact-magazine/2020/voice-treaty-truth/index.html

Secondly, the Bishops' statement also ignores the concerns of several eminent members of the legal profession in Australia who have advanced positions in support of the No case, and this can be seen in the submissions on the proposed constitutional alteration that were made to the federal parliament's Joint Select Committee on the Referendum.

These include former High Court Justice Ian Callinan AM KC, former NSW Court of Appeal Justice Terence Cole KC, former WA Supreme Court Justice Nicholas Hasluck AM KC and the late David Jackson KC (widely considered one the finest constitutional lawyers in Australia).

Their submissions highlight the potential for extensive administrative law litigation arising out of a voice, as well as that a constitutionally enshrined body defined by race, which only Indigenous Australians can vote for or serve in, is inconsistent with the fundamental principle that all citizens are to be treated equally. This principle has its origins in the following statement, found in St Paul's Letter to the Galatians (3: 28): "There is neither Jew nor Gentile, neither slave nor free, nor is there male and female, given you are all one in Christ Jesus."

This is the ultimate Christian statement of the inherent dignity of each person, and implementing this ideal over the last two centuries has been the great calling of the Western liberal democratic tradition.

There is also serious concern about the effect of the proposed Voice among constitutional law academics.

In a submission to the Referendum Inquiry, two of Australia's leading constitutional law academics, Professors Nicholas Aroney and Peter Gerangelos argue that the Voice will in fact radically change the way we are governed and potentially put so many things in the hands of the Courts. In their view, the Courts here may well follow the Canadian path, where it has been determined that government has a special duty (called a *fiduciary duty*) under the law to indigenous people, thus leading, potentially, to schemes of monetary compensation.[4]

Aboriginal Australians were at times brutally mistreated in our history and many have suffered continuing disadvantage. However, that is not a justification for breaching the principle that all people are equal not only in the eyes of the law, but also, and probably more importantly, in fundamental status. Moreover, as the Shadow Minister for Indigenous Affairs, Senator Jacinta Nampijinpa Price has stated, one cannot escape the threat that a constitutionally enshrined 'Voice' will actually serve to divide Australians on the grounds of ethnicity. It also appears to assume that simply because someone is Indigenous, that person is automatically marginalised. Unfortunately, many members of our society are marginalised.

Allied to the inherent dignity of each person is the ideal that we should be treated not, as Martin Luther King Jr said, based on the colour of our skin but on the content of our character. In other words, simply because one is of a particular race, they are by nature disadvantaged and always in need of special help – the culture of victimhood.

The Catholic Bishops of Australia, indeed all clergy, would do well to read carefully a speech given by Pope St John Paul II during his visit to Australia in 1986.

In the speech, given on November 29 of that year, John Paul II addressed Aboriginal people at Blatherskite Park, Alice Springs, calling on all Australians to seek "a just and proper settlement"

---

4 See Submission 92, The Joint Select Committee on the Aboriginal and Torres Strait Islander Voice Referendum, Parliament of Australia, at https://www.aph.gov.au/ Parliamentary_Business/Committees/Joint/Former_Committees/Aboriginal_and_Torres_Strait_Islander_Voice_Referendum/VoiceReferendum/Submissions

on the Indigenous Affairs question. However, he added a note of caution:

> *The establishment of a new society for Aboriginal people cannot go forward without just and mutually recognized agreements with regard to these human problems, even though their causes lie in the past. The greatest value to be achieved by such agreements, which must be implemented without causing new injustices, is respect for the dignity and growth of the human person [...] You are part of Australia and Australia is part of you.*[5]

Over the last 36 years since that exhortation was given, Australians have heeded John Paul II's call. Indeed, there are 11 members of Aboriginal descent in the Commonwealth Parliament, which is the voice for all of us. Aborigines are part of the wider political system and have been for several generations.

Indeed, the contribution of Aboriginal people to this country has, as John Paul II encouraged us, been joyfully received. Witness the many Indigenous people who speak out so powerfully and effectively in our public life, the now routine acknowledgements of country and presence of the Aboriginal flag alongside the national flag.

Moreover, as John Paul II stated all those years ago, Aboriginal people should reject the idea that they are perpetual victims forever in need of special measures, declaring:

> *You, the Aboriginal people of this country and its cities, must show that you are actively working for your own dignity of life. On your part, you must show that you too can walk tall and command the respect which every human being expects*

---

5 Address Of John Paul II to the Aborigines and Torres Strait Islanders in «Blatherskite Park», Alice Spring (Australia), 29 November 1986, https://www.vatican.va/content/john-paul-ii/en/speeches/1986/november/documents/hf_jp-ii_spe_19861129_aborigeni-alice-springs-australia.html

*to receive from the rest of the human family.*[6]

In other words, he understood that the key to helping the minority of Aborigines who have not adjusted to life in a liberal modern society is to end the obsession with identity, since that is what is causing the most harm. As Gary Johns notes in his book, *The Burden of Culture,*[7] 80 per cent of people of Aboriginal descent today are already integrated into the wider Australian society and are doing well, if belatedly, without a Voice to Parliament, and without Aboriginal policies and programmes.

As John Paul II stated all those years ago, present injustices are not removed by resentment. The dangers of new injustices he spoke of are real in terms of the Voice. It may well not end up being the just and proper settlement that he called for. The Catholic Bishops of Australia would do well to heed his prophetic words.

6 Ibid.

7 Gary Johns, The Burden of Culture (*Quadrant*, 2022).

# 11

# THE "VOICE" REFERENDUM: A CHOICE OF NATIONAL IDENTITY

**Shimon Cowen***

## 1. Introduction

What the content is of the "Voice" for Indigenous Australians, proposed in the national referendum for constitutional enshrinement, is unclear. I have, however, looked at some specific "voices" that have been raised in favour of The Voice, and shall seek to make some analysis and evaluation of them here. They have consequences for (1) the material order of the Australian State and (2) the cultural identity of Australian life. In addition to the content must be considered (3) the "tenor" and totalitzing culture. The tenor and total cultural impact of the "Voice" movement is as significant and consequential as its content.

My analysis and evaluation of "The Voice" derives from a group of universal ethical principles known as the Noahide laws, so-called because they were the basis for the renewal of

---

* Rabbi Dr Shimon Cowen, son of a former Governor General of Australia, Sir Zelman Cowen OBM, is an Australian rabbi and academic. He is Director of the Institute for Judaism and Civilization in Melbourne, Australia.

civilisation after the biblical flood with its survivor, and ancestor of all humanity, Noah. These laws or ethical principles have been ratified by the major faiths and confirmed as the bedrock of civilisation in various statements of the American Congress, the President of the European Union, an Islamic Head of State, King Mohammed VI of Morocco, and an Australian Governor General, and are documented in my book *The Theory and Practice of Universal Ethics – the Noahide Laws*.[1] There are seven Noahide laws, each with widely ramifying detail: (1) belief in the Creator and prohibition of idolatry (2) respect for the Creator and for faith, included in a prohibition of blasphemy (3) sexual morality based on traditional marriage (4) the prohibition of theft and material harm (5) the prohibition of murder (6) orderly processes of justice, which also uphold the framework Noahide laws (7) the proper treatment of animals and nature. This primordial moral covenant with humanity was reiterated at Mt Sinai, as an ethical imperative to all humanity, alongside the Ten Commandments, with which it substantially overlaps. The Noahide laws are the source and enduring core of monotheistic tradition.

## 2. The material identity of the State

The identity of the State – with the Government as its representative – is the authority it possesses as a sovereign owner of its territory. The people legitimate its proprietorship and accord it the exclusive legitimate use of force (through its police and army), to use a formulation of the sociologist Max Weber, to uphold its legislative and judicial functions.

In universal, Noahide law, there are in fact three tiers of ownership, all concurrent, but constituting a hierarchy of levels. Thus, the

1 Shimon Dovid Cowen, *The Theory and Practice of Universal Ethics* (Kehot Publication Society, 2015) 408 pp.

Creator is the ultimate owner – and in this sense, the Sovereign – of the entire earth, which He created, and which belongs to Him. All nations of the world are subordinate to His providence and the moral framework of His laws. The owners in the tier beneath the Creator are the Governments or State structures of nations. They possess sovereign ownership over their own lands. State ownership supervenes over the individual ownerships and property holdings of the State's subjects. That means that, within the framework principles of the Creator, they can levy taxes and make "positive" laws for the property and economic relationships between their individual subjects. They can, in circumstances of public and national need also appropriate the property and conscript the labour (as in military service for national defence), of their subjects. Finally, there is the third tier of ownership, the individual owners who have powers of ownership over their own property, to the extent granted them within the positive civil laws and needs of their Governments, and by the Creator's laws.

Amongst the "voices" which have been raised for the "Voice" movement is the view that the sovereignty of the Australian Government over its territory, namely the continent of Australia, is intrinsically questionable. Reasons given are that European sovereignty was established as the result of an invasion; no treaty was made between the incoming conquerors and the aboriginals; and that, in the words of the "Uluru Statement from the Heart", Aboriginal "ownership of the soil" and "sovereignty" within Australia "has never been ceded or extinguished, and coexists with the sovereignty of the Crown". The statement has general significance, as we shall explore, apart from being the source for claims to entitlements, compensation, and land-rights potentially over the whole of Australia.

By contrast, it is explained in Noahide law that the conquest of a land by another nation confers ownership of the conquered land upon the Government of the conquering nation. This is a practical and legal result, irrespective of the ethical character of the conquest – whether the land was taken rightly or wrongly, aggressively or as the result of a war which started defensively. Indeed, it is a nearly, if not wholly, universal phenomenon that states all over the world have generally displaced earlier nations or groupings and occupied their territories. After the event of conquest and the establishment of a new State on the conquered territory, with the practical submission and acceptance of its subjects, the state becomes its owner. To challenge such a state's sovereignty is like challenging the sovereignty of any other existing state. As sovereign proprietor, the laws it makes relating to property within its jurisdiction – so long as these not capricious, arbitrary and inconsistent – are law.

The celebrated "Mabo" case, to my understanding, did not infringe the concept of the sovereignty of the Australian Government – the "Crown" – over Australian territory. Rather, it validated and accorded instances of individual ownership, under the rubric of "native title", to Torres Straits Islanders (and by extension to Aboriginal individuals or communities). It rejected the concept of *terra nullius,* namely that the European conquest of Australia had voided all forms of individual and group ownership prior to British dominion over Australia. In *Mabo* the State, through the court, validated that "title" under specific conditions. The decision did not question, but rather demonstrated Australian sovereignty: native title was *granted* to individuals or groups under and by the Court of the sovereign State. The State could still use its sovereign powers to repossess it, just as it could any individual's property, and to make the rules for the application, designation. and extinguishment of native title.

Current "voices", however, go much further than *Mabo* and individual "native title". They challenge the concept of the sovereignty of the Australian State vis-à-vis the Aboriginal peoples *altogether*. One "voice" in a book compiled by Irene Moores, *Voices of Aboriginal Australia,* states:

> *Australian society must involve recognition of Aboriginal people as indigenous and sovereign; and it must be recognized that every inch of this country has always been related to an Aboriginal nation state. As in the United Nations International Year of the World's Indigenous People, there has to be A New Partnership.*[2]

This chimes with the "Uluru Statement from the Heart" that aboriginal sovereignty over Australia has never been ceded "and coexists with the sovereignty of the Crown". The problem here is that a "divided" sovereignty or a "partnership" of sovereignties within the one territory, are both contradictions in terms. For in such scenarios there is no State, no central legislature, no legitimate monopoly of the means of force, no one set of laws, and ultimately no one authoritative court – that could belong to, and speak for, two separate sovereignties. So long as the Voice is tied to a concept of distinct aboriginal sovereignty, its acceptance must mean that the Australian State must dissolve its *sole* sovereignty. This moves our society towards a conflictual tribalism (as was found in the "Black Lives Matter" movement with its key catchcry "defund the police", the suspension of the State in the exercise of its sovereign authority and proprietorship) unless Australia were to merge into a new sovereign order, the concomitant of a new cultural and spiritual identity.

### 3. Cultural and spiritual identity

Aboriginal claims to sovereignty, in some strong contemporary "voices", are associated with a particular, indigenous "spirituality", as something which claims the allegiance of all Australians. This has been taken up by senior figures among the non-Aboriginal

2 Irene Moores, *Voices of Aboriginal Australia* (Butterfly Books, 1995) 6.

advocates for the Voice. Professor Frank Brennan stated in a recent lecture, "Truth, Treaty and Transformation":

> *Let's always be attentive to the poetry and the symbolism at play in this area of legal and political discourse. The Western Sahara Case was heard by the International Court of Justice in the Hague in the spring of 1975. Let's relish the closing submission by Mr Bayona-Ba-Meya:*
>
> > *'...I have full faith and confidence in the wisdom of the Court ... can only hear and speak the language of nature, which is none other than that of authenticity.'*
>
> *Let's speak the language of nature and authenticity to each other.*[3]

The "language of nature and authenticity" refers to Aboriginal – amongst other forms of indigenous – spirituality. It is instructive to note that advocacy for the Voice fits with a steady and conscious attrition of the Judeo-Christian or monotheistic background of Australian culture. Religion of Judeo-Christian and, for that matter, Islamic heritage is now under attack within Australia – notably in Victoria – where legislation has assumed the right to tell religious schools what they may and what they may not teach of their beliefs to their students. In Victorian State Schools, the one hour of optional weekly religious instruction – whether in Jewish, Christian or Islamic faith – was banned from classroom hours altogether. Thanks to a secularist pressure group, students would now have to come before school or during lunch time to receive that instruction, a deliberate disincentive. In 2008 the so-called Melbourne Declaration, signed by all State and Federal Education Ministers acknowledged the spiritual education of a child as one of the objectives of national education. In fact, it was mentioned

3 Fr Frank Brennan SJ AO, 'Truth, Treaty and Transformation', 2021 Walter Silvester Memorial Lecture, Australian Catholic University, 26 October 2021, at https://www.acu.edu.au/about-acu/institutes-academies-and-centres/pm-glynn-institute/news-and-events/truth-treaty-and-transformation.

three times in the document. In the next revision of the National Curriculum (2014), there was talk of a spirituality component, but one secularly presented as a comparative study to be taught in suspension of religious conviction. In the next version of the National Curriculum in 2021, there was no mention of spirituality at all, with one exception – aboriginal spirituality. As the vestiges or residues are removed from the Australian curriculum, aboriginal spirituality is what is to be taught to *all* Australian students.

Now, Aboriginal religions, like most indigenous religions, are idolatrous. What does that mean? A common definition of idolatry is the location of deity exclusively in natural or created, finite entities and separates them from any connection with a transcendent, sole Creator. This can be in one of two ways: either that there is no concept of a transcendent Creator at all, or that there is one, who yet is believed to have "withdrawn" and have left the management of the world to other powers and forces. The former vests deity in natural entities and spirits, without any mention of an ultimate transcendent deity. The primacy of aboriginal spirituality in education blends with the "religion of nature" which is what certain forms of environmentalism (such as the "deep ecology" of Arne Naess) have become.

Aboriginal spirituality, with its nature deities, is at direct variance with the monotheistic religious tradition embodied in the Judeo-Christian tradition, which acknowledges a transcendent Creator. The patent question is why the children of parents who subscribe to monotheistic faiths should be exposed to a culture of nature worship at the same time as monotheistic faith and teaching is purged from public education. Why is a spirituality which, in the sights of Judeo-Christian or Abrahamic tradition, is idolatrous and pagan – though its adherents are to be fully respected as human beings – made the default spirituality of what has been a monotheistic society?

Idolatrous or pagan societies also possess concomitant values which are directly at variance with those of monotheistic tradition. Though this will not be taught in schools, and it certainly invites the full fury of censorship to say so, traditional Aboriginal society was also associated with much violence. Professor Bill Rubinstein has documented in a number of articles, published in *Quadrant Magazine* over the last year or so, that aboriginal society extensively practised infanticide.[4] Whether due to the cumbersome requirements of carrying a number of children or shortages of food, it was in many places standard practice to cull or kill the additional children, already born or in infancy, which they felt could not be sustained. In addition to this we find amongst some Aboriginal tribes a traditional culture of cannibalism. Conceivably infanticide and cannibalism are no longer practised by aboriginals, but it has roots in a pagan and idolatrous culture. However subliminal the association of pagan idolatry with this kind of killing may be (and even if it is not practised now), a pagan disregard for life (expressed in infanticide) goes all too well with – and can be readily assimilated to – the contemporary culture of killing, expressed in mass abortion on demand and euthanasia, found in our society. It became possible with the attrition of the Judeo-Christian ethic, which repudiates the culture of killing. Starkly and briefly put, is the Voice also about the paganisation and replacement of what has been the Judeo-Christian, Abrahamic or Noahide tradition with its values?

4 William D. Rubinstein, 'Infanticide in Traditional Aboriginal Society', *Quadrant Magazine*, 13 January 2022, at https://quadrant.org.au/magazine/2021/12/infanticide-in-traditional-aboriginal-society/. See also: Rubin D. Rubinstein, 'Life and Death in Pre-Contact Aboriginal Australia', *Quadrant Online*, 18 November 2020, at https://quadrant.org.au/magazine/2020/10/life-and-death-in-pre-contact-aboriginal-australia/.

## 4. The tenor and totalizing culture of the Voice

We are living in an epoch, which I characterized in my book *Politics and Universal Ethics* (and have further elaborated in its sequel, *A Populism of the Spirit – Further Essays on Politics and Universal Ethics*), as a culture of "hedonistic materialism", in which human interests are characterized primarily as a calculus of pleasure and pain and where the human being is grasped primarily as emotive and driven by impulse and feeling. The corollary of this is diminution in the reflective and spiritual faculties of personality. The bodily dimension is primary. The role of reflective, critical reason is diminished inasmuch as it is a limiter on instinctual gratification. Even more repressed is the concept of "conscience", or in religious language, the "soul", which is a source of values and functions – as conscience – as a counterweight to mere impulse. In the Voice movement, there is high tenor of emotion around the buzzword of "reconciliation". What is widely absent is self-reflection, critique and analysis. The consequences, including possible negative consequences of implementation of the "Voice" for aboriginals and non-aboriginals alike, are pushed from consideration as dampeners on the euphoric buzz of "reconciliation". The same happened in the same-sex marriage debate. Consideration of possible consequences such as, and pre-eminently, constriction of religious freedom, were pushed out of consideration by its advocates. It was all about "love" and no more. In fact, the consequences were massive: gender ideology invaded child education with consequences for "transitioning" of children that can no longer be ignored, and a wholesale repression of religious freedoms were set in train through legislation. The transmission of religious beliefs was criminalized as the State moved into religious schools, communities and congregations with gaol sentences and informing. The pro-Voice movement suggests similar characteristics: it is about feeling and feeling brooks no analysis or reflective critique.

Another feature, which the Voice movement has in common with the gender ideology launched by same-sex marriage movement is that it did not stop with accommodating the perceived victim alongside the professing of other social norms. Rather the social norm was inverted so that society should be made identical to the perceived victim. To accommodate the homosexual and the gender dysphoric individual, gender fluidity or genderlessness became the default position of the culture as a whole, as now evidenced in birth certificates (parent 1 and parent 2) and wedding certificates (partner 1 and partner 2) and with children being taught gender fluidity from kindergarten onwards. The perceived victim's culture becomes universal and dominant. Both movements are totalising.

I wish to argue here that with the Voice Referendum we have the same possibility: that instead of the traditional monotheistic Judeo-Christian society with its attendant values, the society *as a whole* is intended to receive the identity of the stylized and idealised pristine indigenous morality of the purported "victim", in the form of a standardised neo-Paganism for society from education right through to forms of public ceremony. As such, in the radical questioning of the sovereignty of Australian Government, there opens up the possibility of unknown conflict with the tribalisation of the Australian State.

This choice in the Voice Referendum is for, and impacts, non-aboriginals and aboriginals alike. It is about the choice of worldview which will best actualise and advance all human beings living in Australia – all of them, as monotheistic tradition puts it, made in the "image of the Divine". The choice is between a society built on Judeo-Christian or Abrahamic or more generally Noahide principles and a neo-Pagan culture, an indigenisation of modernity – co-formed, and perhaps even primarily so, by non-Aboriginals – with its own value set. Most Aboriginals, it would seem, are not attached to older Aboriginal beliefs and in fact have embraced the Judeo-Christian tradition and society, to the extent that religion plays a role in their lives. They, and non-aboriginal Australians too, must ask themselves, whether they want a monotheistic or a neo-Pagan identity for Australia.

# 12

# MORAL IMPLICATIONS OF THE VOICE FOR AUSTRALLIA

**John Fleming***

## 1. Introduction

There have always been those who appeal to their Christian Faith to justify the decisions they make on quite other grounds. For example, Voice campaigner Greg Craven says,

> *The voice is a great moral imperative. Anyone who believes this has no choice but to support it. For me,* ***the moral logic of the voice flows deeply from my Catholic faith****. All people are given life by a loving God, who demands they be able to live it to the fullest. It is clear to me that Indigenous people never have had that right, and still do not have it.*[1] *[emphasis added]*

Craven is right when he describes the Voice issue as a moral issue, but wrong when he opines (without any supportive argumentation) that support for the Voice "flows deeply from" the Catholic faith.

---

* Fr John Fleming PhD is a well published author and academic, specialising in medical ethics, political philosophy, and the fundamental requirements of good public policy. He was a foundation member of UNESCO's International Bioethics Committee and an elected delegate to the Australian Constitutional Convention 1998.

1 Greg Craven, "Why I will join Julian Leeser in Indigenous voice to parliament Yes push, *The Australian*, 20 April 2023.

Nothing could be further from the truth. Sentimentality does not trump basic moral principles.

Personal disclosure: I have long been a supporter of including a reference to Indigenous Australians in The Preamble to the Australian Constitution. In February 1998 I moved the following motion at the Constitutional Convention.

> *That this Working Group, representing a wide range of opinion on the republic, recommends to the Constitutional Convention:*
>
> *that the Preamble should include recognition of Aboriginal peoples and Torres Strait Islanders as the original inhabitants of Australia who enjoy equally with all other Australians fundamental human rights.*[2]

## 2. The argument

In this short essay I will present the fundamental teachings of the Catholic Church where the political arrangements of the State are concerned.

1. I will identify some of the relevant **Biblical texts** which form the theological basis of Catholic social teaching.
2. I will explain **the essential elements of Church teaching,** based on the scriptural texts, as those teachings have developed over the centuries, and which are crucial to a morally sound set of constitutional arrangements for the state. The three key principles where the current debate is concerned are:
    a. The principle of participation,
    b. The principle of solidarity/interdependence,

2 *Constitutional Convention, Transcript of Proceedings, Hansard*, 6 February 1998, 431

and

c. The principle of subsidiarity.

### 3. The Biblical texts - what do they tell us about human nature?

The first book in the Bible:

> *God created mankind in his own image, in the image of God he created them;* ***male and female he created them.***[3] *[emphasis added]*

From this text arise the doctrines of the inherent dignity of the human being and the equal and inalienable rights of all human beings about which there is now universal agreement.[4]

> *Considering that, in accordance with the principles proclaimed in the Charter of the United Nations, recognition of the inherent dignity and of the equal and inalienable rights of all members of the human family is the foundation of freedom, justice and peace in the world,*
>
> *Recognizing that these rights derive from the inherent dignity of the human person,*[5]

The major author of the Universal Declaration of Human Rights, Nobel Prize winner René Cassin,[6] "locates the ideological roots of the Declaration in the Ten Commandments."[7]

---

3 *Genesis* 1:27

4 Cf the *Universal Declaration of Human Rights*, 1948

5 From the Preamble in the *International Covenant on Civil and Political Rights*, 1967

6 John Warwick Montgomery, *Human Rights and Human Dignity*, Dallas: Probe Books, 1986, 26. Cassin, assisted by Karel Vasak, founded the International Institute of Human Rights, Strasbourg, France.

7 Ibid., 30

This teaching about the radical equality of human beings, male and female, did not just apply to fellow Jews, but to everyone, as the book of Leviticus instructs.

> *When a foreigner resides among you in your land, do not mistreat them.*
>
> ***The foreigner residing among you must be treated as your native-born.*** *Love them as yourself, for you were foreigners in Egypt. I am the LORD your God.*[8] *[Emphasis added]*

St Paul explicates this teaching with even greater specificity in terms of the Gospel of Jesus Christ:

> *There is neither Jew nor Gentile, neither slave nor free, nor is there male and female, for you are all one in Christ Jesus.*[9]

### 4. Principles of Social Order

Drawing upon the Old and New Testaments of the Bible, the Church has identified several crucial principles upon which to construct the democratic political community.

*Participation*

From the Old Testament it can be seen that "I am my brother's keeper".[10] We are responsible for each other, which is to say that we have obligations for the welfare of others. In any community of human beings, different people have different gifts, abilities, and responsibilities. We need each other. From this interdependence the response must be a moral response, a commitment to the

8 *Leviticus* 19: 33-34

9 *Galatians* 3:28 and cf also *Psalm* 67:4 "May the nations be glad and sing for joy, for you rule the peoples with equity and guide the nations of the earth."

10 Cf *Genesis* 4:9

common good, to the good of all and of each individual. This moral response is called solidarity.[11]

*Solidarity*

Solidarity is not the equivalence of a vague sense of compassion or shallow distress at the misfortunes of others. It is about the recognition of each other as persons.

> *Within each society ... those who are more influential ... should feel responsible for the weaker ... Those who are weaker ... should not adopt a purely passive attitude ... but, while claiming their legitimate rights, should do what they can for the good of all.*[12]

*Subsidiarity*

The principle of subsidiarity is best described in these terms:

> ***What individuals can accomplish by their own initiative and efforts should not be taken from them by a higher authority.*** *A greater and higher social institution must not take over the duties of a subordinate organization and deprive it of its competence. Its purpose, rather, is to intervene in a subsidiary fashion (thus offering help) when individuals or smaller institutions find that a task is beyond them.*[13] *[emphasis added]*

For example, a local Aboriginal community wishes to control the incidences of violence, sexual abuse of women and children, and related issues. It wants their area to be declared an alcohol-free zone by the banning of the sale and purchase of alcoholic drinks

11 Pope Saint John Paul II, *Sollicitudo Rei Socialis*, 1987, "The "Concern of the Church for the Social Order".

12 Pope Saint John Paul II, *ibid.*

13 Spirit and Life, 'Youcat – Catholic Faith and Cathechism for the Youth', Question n. 323, at https://spiritandeternallife.blogspot.com/2017/07/youcat-commented-through-ccc-question-n_26.html.

in that area. State, Territory, and Federal Governments intervene to prevent that local community to have its wishes respected. The principle of subsidiarity requires that the wishes of the local community to overcome local problems must be respected by those exercising "higher authority".

## 5. Western culture

The genius of Western civilisation/culture is the achievement of the interaction of Jerusalem, Athens, and Rome.

From Jerusalem "the West" learned that life is an adventure, a journey, a pilgrimage. Martin Luther King made much of the Exodus story in his campaign for equal recognition under the law for all Americans, black, white or any other description.

Greek classical philosophy taught us that:

1. there are truths, inscribed into the world and into us, and which may be discerned by human beings.
2. we can know those truths by reason; and, where morality is concerned, we come to know our obligations to ourselves and to others.
3. that logic requires acceptance of the principle of noncontradiction, that a proposition cannot both be true and untrue at the same time when dealing with the same context.[14]

It is beyond the scope of this short essay to discuss this further here. But it is unquestionably true that Catholic Christianity has been crucial in shaping western civilisation as we have received it in Australia. Western civilisation is not just the personal subjective possession of individuals who subjectively refer to "my Catholic

14 George Weigel, Foreword to Joseph Cardinal, *Western Culture Today and Tomorrow: Addressing Fundamental Issues,* Ignatius Press, Kindle Edition, 2019.

faith", as does Craven. It is a reality which objectively stands independently of private opinion, current social obsessions, or political populism.

### 6. Aboriginal and Torres Strait Islander peoples have a share in Western civilisation.

Australian indigenous peoples have also received the great treasures of Western Christian civilisation. Where personal religious belief is concerned, the 2016 Census showed that there were broad similarities in the religious affiliation of Australia's Aboriginal and Torres Strait Islander population and the non-Indigenous population.

Overall, 54 per cent of Aboriginal and Torres Strait Islander peoples reported a Christian affiliation, almost the same proportion as the non-Indigenous population (55%).

In 2016, less than 2 per cent of the Aboriginal and Torres Strait Islander population reported adherence to Australian Aboriginal Traditional religions or beliefs. This has remained steady over the last 20 years.[15] Christianity is now a crucial part of indigenous cultures whether secularists like it or not. For example, the chairman of the Torres Strait eastern islands and elder statesman from the island of Erubam Le, George Mye, said this at the Australian Constitutional Convention (1998).

> *The arrival at Darnley, or Erub, Island in 1871 by the first Christian missionaries of the London Missionary Society had a profound influence over customs, tradition and society in the Torres Strait, the most notable being the 'Coming of the Light'—the establishment of Christianity throughout*

15 At the Australian Bureau of Statistics, https://www.abs.gov.au/ausstats/abs@.nsf/Lookup/by%20Subject/2071.0~2016~Main%20Features~Religion%20Article~80.

*the Torres Strait region. The Queen became the head of our church and central to the religious, cultural and civic traditions of the people of the Torres Strait.*[16]

Australia as a nation is part of the strong cultural legacy which has determined the way a democratic society should organise itself.

## 7. Why the Voice should be rejected

1. First, *it is contrary to the principle of solidarity.* The Voice introduces a governing structure into the Australian Constitution, participation in which is based upon belonging to a particular race or ethnicity. Special rights and privileges will be awarded to persons based upon racial identity.
2. *It is also contrary to the principle of participation.* "It is necessary that all participate, each according to his position and role, in promoting the common good. This obligation is inherent in the dignity of the human person." This principle requires the participation of local communities in decisions which most closely affect them. The State enacts legislation to protect the interests, needs, of those local groups. It is not for the Voice to have a controlling say over Federal legislation, and especially since the Federal Parliament already has elected members who are indigenous persons. This is a crucial part of Western Christian civilisation. The Voice will be comprised only of people of a particular race who do not necessarily reflect the wishes of Indigenous peoples because they will not have been elected by the members of that community. **They are appointees**

16 George Mye, *Speech to the Constitutional Convention 2nd to 13th February 1998*, Old Parliament House, Canberra, ACT, Hansard Transcript of Proceedings, the 2nd of February 1998, 73.

**with privilege.** "It is necessary that all participate, each according to his position and role, in promoting the common good. This obligation is inherent in the dignity of the human person."[17]

3. *The Voice is contrary to the principle of subsidiarity.* It is by no means clear that its membership will include significant numbers of Indigenous people living in rural and remote areas, and who have the greatest need for support in the legislative programmes of the State. Inner city dwelling secularist intellectuals, representing only themselves, many of whom promote the cultural Marxist agenda which exploits race as evidence of a culture of the repressed and the repressor, really do not identify with those who live in poverty, those whose family life is constantly disrupted if not destroyed by extreme violence and sexual abuse.
4. The present system of voting for individuals to represent the people in the Parliament has provided a greater proportion of politicians identifying as indigenous than their proportion in the wider community. This is not a problem because that is the democratic will of all voters casting their votes, not based on race or colour, but on perceived merit.

## 8. Solidarity and race relations

Previous attempts of governments in Australia to vest power in newly created government structures have been less than successful in promoting any sense of solidarity between Australians of different racial backgrounds. In the past, those structures as creatures of Federal legislation could be abolished. And they were, because they were seen as the occasions of the exacerbation

17 *Catechism of the Catholic Church*, n. 1913.

of racial differences, corruption, and had no appreciable effect in promoting the welfare of indigenous peoples.

The Voice is, and will be, in the same tradition only this time Federal Parliament will not have the independent power to control it, let alone abolish it. Structures like the Voice necessarily exaggerate the differences between the groups they claim to represent and the nation. In short, as an appointed group with privilege, they will not advance the common good of the nation, the common good of all, or even the good of the peoples they claim to represent.

Rather than encouraging reconciliation, what we will see is a deepening of the divide between Indigenous peoples and the wider community. One advocate of the Voice, Marcia Langton, a former member of the Communist Party (a political commitment that she seems not to have rejected), has promised Australians a deepening of the race divide if they don't vote for the Voice.

> *When Australians go to the polls to vote on the Voice later this year, Langton wants them to think hard about what's at stake. "I imagine that most Australians who are non-Indigenous, if we lose the referendum, will not be able to look me in the eye," she says. "**How are they going to ever ask an Indigenous person, a Traditional Owner, for a welcome to country?** How are they ever going to be able to ask me to come and speak at their conference? If they have the temerity to do it, of course the answer is going to be no."*[18]

Indigenous peoples who have descended from long past generations who had sole occupancy of the land maintained the traditional belief that man's relationship to the land was not ownership but connection. It is not "owned" by any one person or group. On the contrary it is shared with particular groups

18 Helen Trinca, "Vote 'No' and you won't get a welcome to country again", *The Weekend Australian Magazine*, 8 April 2023.

having responsibility to care for certain sections of the Australian continent. It should be noted that the present rhetoric moves away from being traditionally "connected" [19] to the land, to traditional "ownership" of the land now espoused by Marcia Langton.

The Voice and the politics of "ownership" of the land represents a significant move towards the claim for "treaty" which, if successful, would mean two countries in one, with indigenous people having a say in the running of the country not considered to be "theirs" as well as the one considered to be "theirs" and in whose name the treaty would be signed. The question is already there with the "welcome to country" in which representatives of the very few welcome Australians to their own country.

All of this necessarily will contribute to a deeper division of Australians because of race, of colour.

The Western tradition to which indigenous people give free allegiance is that expressed in a tradition going back more than two and a half thousand years and to which more than half of Aboriginal and Torres Strait Islanders belong. That some key promoters of the Voice are at war with fundamental elements of Western Christian civilisation should be made clearer than is the case in the current debate.

> ***The foreigner residing among you must be treated as your native-born.*** *Love them as yourself, for you were foreigners in Egypt. I am the LORD your God.*[20] *[Emphasis added]*

Christianity, the shared religion of the majority of Australians, indigenous or not, has provided important principles to the

19 Cf "Evolve Communities acknowledges the Traditional Owners and their continuing connection to land, sea and community …",at https://www.evolves.com.au/our_approach/.

20 *Leviticus* 19: 33-34.

way in which Western nations have evolved. The Voice would, if accepted, undermine essential features of Western cultural civilisation, deepen racial divisions in Australia, and endow persons with a particular "racial identity" with special rights and privileges not accorded to the vast majority of Australians.

# 13

# OUR COMMON HUMANITY AND THE SEARCH FOR TRUTH

**David Daintree***

*But as many as received him, to them gave he power to become the sons of God, even to them that believe on his name: Which were born, not of blood, nor of the will of the flesh, nor of the will of man, but of God.*[1]

Having been asked by your editors to contribute a chapter on the 'no' case for the Voice from 'a predominantly religious perspective', my first impulse was to explore the views of Church leaders who are presumably well formed in the principles of Christian ethics.

This was to prove unhelpful. On 3 July 2022 a Mass was celebrated in North Sydney to inaugurate the Church's long-awaited Plenary Council. Many of the Australian Bishops were present. Given the long lead-time (the Plenary had been at least two years in the planning), and the wide range of representation by both clergy and laity, one should have been entitled to expect that the mind of the Church on vital moral and theological issues would be fully manifest. It's a worrying thought that in the event perhaps it was.

---

* David Daintree is director of the Christopher Dawson Centre for Cultural Studies in Tasmania, Australia. He has a background in Classics and teaches Late and Medieval Latin. Daintree was a visiting professor at the universities of Siena and Venice, and a visiting scholar at the University of Manitoba. He served as President of Campion College from 2008 to 2012.

1 John 1:12-3.

The first ten minutes of the Mass were devoted to an Aboriginal 'smoking ceremony', a purportedly religious practice dating back to the 70s of the twentieth century, accompanied by the plangent music of the didgeridoo. Much more importantly, and of enormous theological significance, there followed an invocation of 'male and female spirits' by a woman who was introduced as an elder of the indigenous community.

The suitability of the music is not at issue: the choice of an Aboriginal instrument is unexceptionable, given that the organ, the only instrument specifically designated for purposes of worship, has long since been displaced by the guitar. The Catholic Church in this country is not noted for the high quality of its music, generally preferring songs of little musical or theological merit. Few Catholics seem aware anymore that musicians like Haydn and Mozart were also Catholic, and that they wrote hymns. It would therefore be unreasonable and hypocritical to take exception to the use of aboriginal music. In fact, the didgeridoo produced an attractive sound, perhaps somewhat repetitive and unmemorable, but quaintly evocative and 'atmospheric', and certainly much more appealing than the folksy stuff we usually hear from the Church PA system.

But the invocation of spirits is quite another matter. That practice has always been strictly forbidden and anathematised by the whole Christian Church. The clearest early manifestation of this prohibition is found in the Bible, in the First Book of Samuel, where King Saul secretly consults a witch at Endor, having previously forbidden his subjects to engage in any form of necromancy. This deceit on Saul's part leads to his own downfall and suicide. Such a practice has always been regarded, in both Judaism and Christianity, as an insult to God.

There is no room here for controversy as to the facts and no grounds for denying that the inclusion of this ritual at the start of the Plenary Mass was a completely pagan act. It was pagan, though without the intellectual content or integrity that characterises higher pagan thought. It should never have taken place within a Christian Church. The fact that it did, and that it did so as a sort of preface to the Eucharist, and in the presence of a high proportion of the bishops, is simply staggering.

By this act of sentimental folly, the subsequent deliberations of the Plenary were compromised if not wholly vitiated. The delegates' predictable apologies to all the usual victims, and the strong recommendation that every Sunday Mass in every church in the land should thereafter be preceded by a 'recognition of country', will contribute nothing to the unity and harmony of the nation. If we want an authentic religious perspective on the Voice, the modern Church is not the place to find it.

I do not question the personal integrity of those who conducted the ceremony. Without doubt they passionately valued their aboriginal inheritance and considered its preservation a matter of the highest importance. But the plain, sad truth is that the culture and language of many of the coastal aboriginal tribes is now extinct, and that rituals such as this are largely synthetic and therefore, in a strict sense, spurious. 'My DNA predates Australia,' claimed the lady who presided at the ceremony, and that is no doubt correct. But what DNA? Aboriginal DNA only, or the DNA of all the other people's whose blood flows and blends together in our veins? And what is this 'connection with the Earth' of which we are constantly reminded? Many Australian families of aboriginal and European descent, or both, have lived here for centuries. Is not the land our common home? The congregation was invited to touch the ground, and all obediently complied. A nice gesture perhaps, but hardly appropriate at a Mass that has its focus on Heaven.

An active interest in tracing ancestry has become very popular in recent years, as evidenced by such TV shows as *Who Do You Think You Are?* and by the extensive advertising of firms like *Ancestry.com*. Tracking one's forbears is indeed a fascinating and occasionally addictive exercise, for it exposes the complexity of human physical inheritance and quickly disabuses us of our quaint tendency to follow solely the male line. In the West, at least, the common system of inheritance, known as primogeniture, means that only the senior male counts in a line of succession. This is a curious survival at a time when women's equal rights have long been widely recognised, but it survives because it is simple and easy to follow, even if at the sacrifice of perspective.

A researcher a few years ago reported that the late Queen Elizabeth II was descended 'directly' from Mohammed. Could that be true? It may well be, but if we are bold enough to tear ourselves away from that preoccupation with the male line and do a quick calculation on the back of an envelope, we shall probably find that hundreds of millions of people are descended from Mohammed. The eldest male line is no more significant genetically than any of the other lines of descent that make up our incredibly complex family trees.

When it comes to DNA and the hidden life of atomic and sub-atomic particles, appearances, it seems, can be highly deceptive. The unseen fabric of life, the reality behind appearances, is full of glorious and exciting mystery: every bath you take contains one molecule of water that once laved the comely limbs of Cleopatra.

Our racial identity is likewise almost incredibly complex and all claims to nobility, rank or status based upon descent and breeding are fundamentally absurd. John Ball, the would-be mediaeval reformer (he was executed for his trouble in 1381) famously asked the question:

> *When Adam delved and Eve span,*
> *Who was then the gentleman?*

How preposterous all our claims to social rank and status appear once examined! All claims of so-called racial purity, beloved of Nazis and the Ku Klux Klan, are groundless absurdities. In truth we are all joined together in the common web of humanity. We each have hundreds of direct ancestors, thousands indeed if we track back far enough into the past. If we could search back far enough, we would all find slaves among our ancestors – and slave owners too. It's a hard saying, but if some of us are descended from rape victims, the inevitable, depressing corollary of that is that we are also the offspring of rapists.

Our country must recognise that we have become a melting pot of all nations and races, and that there's good and bad in each one of us, and unwanted skeletons in every closet. It is no more reasonable to impute guilt for the crimes committed against aboriginals (and against convicts too) to the present generation of Australians, most of whom are descended from people who came to this country long after it had been 'invaded' by the first European settlers, than it is to hold modern Europeans responsible for the persecution of the Celts by the Anglo-Saxons, or the Etruscans by the Romans. All peoples on earth have blood on their hands; slavery, tyranny and the greedy theft of other people's land have been practised on every continent. When it comes to lineage, who shall cast the first stone?

In 1967, 56 years ago, a referendum was held to allow a change to the Constitution that would effectively remove the last impediment to the recognition of our aboriginal people as full citizens. Australians are slow to accept constitutional changes, but the 1967 referendum succeeded dramatically – 90.77% voted 'yes'. It was an extraordinary outcome. 1967 was an era of student revolution worldwide. Young people were in ferment. Demonstrations demanding change were frequent and often violent. Everywhere policies were changed, and governments fell in response to passionate radicalism.

But was the 1967 constitutional change just a consequence of youthful zeal? Of course not. A 90% YES vote can only be explained by a huge *cross-generational* shift in thinking. Those of us who were young at the time agreed with the shift, but we hadn't initiated it on our own. It was the fruit of many years of reflection, of the good intentions of a society that wanted to be just and fair.

Half a century later this has mostly been forgotten. You can meet many older people (if you try) who went to school with aboriginal mates and played sport with them. They'll often tell you now that things have changed since those times, and that mutual suspicion has gradually squeezed out friendship. The two communities are actually growing further apart, not closer together as we hoped they would. Billions have been spent, millions have been wasted (or worse), interracial discord has grown more bitter, aboriginals continue to feel neglected, and poorer, white people are becoming increasingly resentful of financial advantages going to fellow citizens who 'identify' as aboriginal.

It's not a pretty picture and it can't end well. You would have to be foolishly naive to imagine that the lead-up to the referendum will not give rise to a great deal of straight talking about the nature and definition of aboriginality, much of which will be castigated as 'hate speech' by those who disagree with it. It will be unpleasant, but necessary. Authentic aboriginals rightly fear that unfounded claims, particularly when used to substantiate applications for funding and other benefits, can hijack their cause.

Our best hope is that we can side-step the Voice, which will lead to endless controversy no matter which side prevails and look for better ways to define and understand ourselves. Fortunately, some aboriginal leaders such as Senator Jacinta Price show us a way forward. When race is the chief criterion for making judgements about spending public monies the result is race-based paternalism, otherwise known as *apartheid*.

No amount of wishing changes facts. The sad truth is that authentic Aboriginal culture is today almost unperceived by Australians who live in our cities and towns, and that there is no aspect of our daily lives that is impacted by it. Even among proponents of the Aboriginal cause few of those who advocate renaming towns and regions take the trouble actually to learn an Aboriginal language. Many of those languages are in any case now extinct. According to the last census about 5% of the population claims to 'identify' as Aboriginal, which corresponds very closely to the proportion of Aboriginal members of parliament who already have and exercise a Voice. We have not yet reached the stage of applying the term 'cultural appropriation' to those who seek advantage by claiming indigeneity on the basis of little or no Aboriginal ancestry, but that will surely come.

Where to from here? Annual re-enactments of Governor Arthur Phillip's landing at Sydney Cove, once common enough on Australia Day, 26 January, are a thing of the past. It would be both foolish and insensitive to bring them back. But the events of that day, and their significance for the unfolding of Australia's future, cannot be forgotten or denied. After decades of immigration. the proportion of Aboriginal DNA in Australia's gene pool is growing smaller with each passing year, but the foundational part Aboriginals played in our nation, sometimes tragic, sometimes noble, deserves to be remembered too. Nobody alive today is guilty of the sins of previous generations. We ought to honour both traditions, and disparage neither, but the Voice is not the instrument we need.

If the referendum fails, enormous and bitter disappointment will follow: a defeat would be a deeply sad psychological blow to those honest and honourable members of the aboriginal community who have been led to set their hearts upon a new victory. It is hard to see harmony emerging from an emotional morass of dashed hopes and shattered dreams, but that does not justify voting 'yes' out of sympathy, for misplaced kindness based on unsubstantiated sentiment surely cannot lead to resolution.

Our search for a 'religious perspective' comes down to no more than as search for truth. We began this chapter with words of the Evangelist St John, for whom the different grades or manners of human ancestry count as nothing. Adoption by God is all that counts, a view I would suggest that accords well with most if not all of the world's religions. Now this mode of thinking, we might suppose, will count for little with unbelievers, whether raised in the Christian tradition or not. And yet, does not even the staunchest atheist insist on the *brotherhood* of mankind? There is common ground here, for people of good will.

We close with another scriptural reference in which the Psalmist talks about the human *telos*, our ultimate goal and completion. Nothing here about race, or family, or proportionality, or even equity in the strict legal sense. We must have clean hands, even if our forefathers didn't always, we must avoid vain presumptions, and we must be truthful...

> *The earth is the LORD'S, and the fulness thereof; the world, and they that dwell therein.*
>
> *For he hath founded it upon the seas, and established it upon the floods.*
>
> *Who shall ascend into the hill of the LORD? or who shall stand in his holy place?*
>
> *He that hath clean hands, and a pure heart; who hath not lifted up his soul unto vanity, nor sworn deceitfully.*[2]

2 Ps xxiv, 1-4.

# 14

# NOT SORRY AND SHOULD NOT BE

**Matthew Littlefield***

With all of the talk at the moment regarding the proposal of The Voice to Parliament, it is important for Australians to reflect on what they are being told about the moral status of their existence in this great southern land. Often, we are told that we should be sorry and that we should be doing more to make up for the "injustice" of European settlement in Australia. We are being informed, rather patronisingly, by politicians, the media, especially academia and even segments of the Church, that the proposed change to the Constitution, to create a permanent Indigenous voice in the parliament of Australia, is a necessary step to move towards atoning for the "original sin" of settlement. But is this really an "original sin"? Should we be perpetually sorry? How should we think about this?

Firstly, you should never be expected to say sorry for what someone else has done. Now that this simple and plain bit of wisdom is out of the way, let's go further on this issue.

Why does our culture, and not only our culture, but the prevailing progressive culture across the West, put so much emphasis on

---

* Rev. Matthew Littlefield is an ordained Baptist minister, a regular columnist for Caldron Pool and The Good Sauce, and a published author. All biblical references are from the ESV translation of the Bible.

telling the descendants of colonial powers that they should be sorry for living in these abundant and wonderful lands? Again and again, we are told how sorry we should be, how we should have a sorry day, how if you don't feel sorry you are a terrible person. Why does this happen? Because this is a direct inversion of what we should be doing, and our culture is currently overlorded by an evil ideology; and what does evil always do? It subverts.

Not only should we not be sorry about living in modern Australia, but we should also actually be thankful, hopeful and watchful. We should be thankful that God gave us this land. We should be hopeful of the good things our nation could be, going forward. And we should be watchful to make sure that we do not fall into sinful depravity, because we know that if we do, God may decide to punish us, as he has many other people throughout history. We learn these principles both from the Bible and from the history of our people, the Anglo-Saxons.

The Bible provides a deep theology of dispossession. It teaches us that God owns all the land, everywhere, "The earth is the Lord's and the fullness thereof, the world and those who dwell within" (Psalm 24:1). This is the first pillar of this theology. No people on earth, whether pagan or Christian, homeowner or national sovereign, should view their land as anything more than a stewardship. God shows us very clearly in his own Scriptures how he takes lands from wicked peoples and gives them to new peoples. You might be thinking immediately of the Israelites. But if you read Deuteronomy 2 to 3 you will see that God does this for other nations as well. He worked through the Edomites and Moabites to punish the former inhabitants of the lands he gave them to steward.

But God also does this for his own people. We read in Leviticus 25:23: "The land shall not be sold in perpetuity, for the land is mine. For you are strangers and sojourners with me. 24 And in all the country you possess, you shall allow a redemption of the land." Accordingly, the land the Israelites inhabited was only theirs to steward, they were not the owners of it.[1] They were also warned that if they lived wickedly, God would take it from them (Deut. 28). The Israelites only had the land under the condition they lived as God's people,

> *8 You shall therefore keep the whole commandment that I command you today, that you may be strong, and go in and take possession of the land that you are going over to possess, 9 and that you may live long in the land that the Lord swore to your fathers to give to them and to their offspring, a land flowing with milk and honey (Deut. 11:8-9).*

At many points the Bible emphasises that those who inhabit the land of Israel were nothing more than stewards of God's land. But this theology extends far beyond the Israelites. It applied also to the Canaanites and Amorites and other people's whose land was given to the Hebrews. This teaching in emphasised from Moses to Jesus throughout the Bible.

These passages allow us to build a theology of dispossession. God owns the land, he grants usage of the land to a particular people or nation, and he expects those people to live up to a certain standard. If they do not, he will take the land from them and give it to someone else. This happens again and again in the Bible, and throughout history.

History also shows us that Christian nations had this same view in the past. A good example comes from Bede's Ecclesiastical History of England. Written by Bede in 731, this book gives us the history of the conversion of the English people to Christianity. In fact, Bede, and through him, the Church, give us our first complete and written understanding of the English people. He begins his history

1 Jesus reiterates this with several parables in the New Testament.

by reference to the original people of the land, the Britons, who existed there before the Romans. His perspective, as an Anglo-Saxon, of the Britons is scathing. This is what he observes:

> *When however, the ravages of the enemy at length ceased, the island began to abound with such plenty of grain as had never been known in any age before; with plenty, luxury increased, and this was immediately attended with all sorts of crimes; in particular, cruelty, hatred of truth, and love of falsehood; insomuch, that if any one among them happened to be milder than the rest, and inclined to truth, all the rest abhorred and persecuted him, as if he had been the enemy of his country. Nor were the laity only guilty of these things, but even our Lord's own flock, and his pastors also, addicting themselves to drunkenness, animosity, litigiousness, contention, envy, and other such like crimes, and casting off the light yoke of Christ. In the meantime, on a sudden, a severe plague fell upon that corrupt generation, which soon destroyed such numbers of them, that the living were scarcely sufficient to bury the dead: yet, those that survived, could not be withdrawn from the spiritual death, which their sins had incurred, either by the death of their friends, or the fear of their own. Whereupon, not long after, a more severe vengeance, for their horrid wickedness, fell upon the sinful nation. They consulted what was to be done, and where they should seek assistance to prevent or repel the cruel and frequent incursions of the northern nations; and they all agreed with their King Vortigern to call over to their aid, from the parts beyond the sea, the Saxon nation; which, as the event still more evidently showed, appears to have been done by the appointment of our Lord Himself, that evil might fall upon them for their wicked deeds.*[2]

2 The Venerable Bede, *The Ecclesiastical History of the English People* [731] (Neeland Media LLC), 21.

Bede here is describing how a wealthy and prosperous people, living at ease, became corrupted and fell into depravity and decadence. And because of this, God judged them. But the more frightful punishment he brought was not the plague, but their dispossession from their own lands. God judged the Britons with the invaders that they had allowed to come in, even invited, and handed the land of the Britons to the Angles and the Saxons.

> *In short, the fire kindled by the hands of these pagans proved God's just revenge for the crimes of the people; not unlike that which, being once lighted by the Chaldeans, consumed the walls and city of Jerusalem. For the barbarous conquerors acting here in the same manner, or rather the just Judge ordaining that they should so act, they plundered all the neighbouring cities and country, spread the conflagration from the eastern to the western sea, without any opposition, and covered almost every part of the devoted island.*[3]

The view of Bede was that the Britons had abandoned God, and therefore were dispossessed by the hand of God, through the Anglo-Saxons. This was the standard view of the Church throughout most of Christian history, and it is also the teaching of the Scriptures. But added to this is the idea that the new people in the land stand under the precise same warning. They too must hold to faithfulness in God, otherwise they too will be removed from sovereignty in their land, or even outright possession of their land. They cannot become proud and arrogant and think they are better than those they dispossessed, because if they do, they will simply face the same fate.

This theology places us as stewards under the humble authority of God. It encourages us to live well in the land, but also warns us not to let prosperity corrupt us. Whereas a theology of "sorry", places us in a humanistic ideology, which says that the people

3 Ibid.

who were previously here are of the land, and anyone else who comes in is just an invader, always, and must feel guilty about this in perpetuity. This is not a biblical theology of land ownership, and it is pagan. And much of the church has taken on this way of thinking and called it erroneously, "advocating for justice."

But justice for whom?

No one today perpetrated the dispossession. We are the descendants of those who came. And all Australians live now in a beautiful land and can prosper if they set their mind to it. In fact, many Australians are now the combined descendants of the Indigenous and the British settlers; we have been intertwined, and speaking of separate destinies now is no longer a simple issue. We should not be sorry about living in the current Australia, but rather we should be exceedingly thankful. We live in a land that has been blessed with much. We should be thankful that God has allowed us to live in such a country, and thankful for the great abounding plains he has afforded to all Australians; and thankful that we can have a bright future if we so choose.

But we should also be humble. We should not celebrate the fact that the previous stewards of this land have been dispossessed. We should be watchful that we do not reject righteous living otherwise we too will be dispossessed. In fact, I would argue that this process has already begun. Australians are losing their land to an increasingly large supply of immigrants from very alien cultures that in many ways are objectively opposed to our way of life; and, at the same time, we see the rise of the concept of giving the land back to the descendants of the older inhabitants of this land and increasing moves to go further on this issue. Nations that lose their sovereignty often regain it, after some time, especially when those who took it from them start to degenerate in culture. And Australia is seriously degenerating in culture. In fact, I would argue that all the talk about "sorry" is a false spirituality that has been designed to cloud over how Australians should really think about themselves in this land: as stewards who are here at the pleasure of the King of Kings, which, remember, our Constitution acknowledges in its very Preamble.

None of this wipe away all the pain and suffering that nations feel about losing their own lands and their self-rule. It is understandable to feel deep pain about the situation. I have Slavic and English ancestors, and both those peoples were brutally conquered by others at various points in their history, especially the Slavs – look up what happened to the Slavic world under the Mongols and various German peoples. It is the way of this world for nations to rise and fall, and then to rise again in typically diminished glory. But what a nation must never do is forget who our true God is – the Lord God – and how we should live in His land. Because if we do forget that I dare to inform that God will discipline us. He has done it consistently throughout history, and I strongly suspect Australians are facing this possibility today.

May we repent as a nation of false spiritualities and turn again to the Lord.

# 15

# JOHN RAWLS AND THE ABORIGINAL QUESTION

**Paul Collits***

It has been said, on more than one occasion, that most Aborigines have never even heard of the proposal for "the Voice". This might be considered alarming but, on reflection, it is not remotely unexpected. This is all anecdotal, because, as far as I am aware, no one has formally asked the Indigenous peoples of Australia – everyday Aborigines, as opposed to activists – what they think of the Voice, or of our existing democratic institutions to which they have unbridled access and equal rights of influence.

This gives rise to a larger question, namely, what do Indigenous Australians – for Australians we all are – think about their collective circumstances two hundred and a bit years after the arrival of Captain Arthur Phillip and his convicts and officials? If Aborigines in, say 1787, had been asked – and if they had understood the question – what kind of life they would choose to be living, in, say 2023, I wonder what most of them would have said. Would they have been open to the whole British deal? The

---

* Paul Collits is a freelance writer and independent researcher who has worked in government, industry and the university sector. He has taught at tertiary level in three different disciplines - politics, geography and planning and business studies.

one that the Maori chiefs chose across the Ditch. The answers of our Indigenous people might have been surprising.

It so happens that asking such a question has been a standard device of Western philosophers since the time of Thomas Hobbes and John Locke. Which brings us to the late John Rawls, an esteemed Harvard philosopher of the late twentieth century, and his theory of the just polity.

## 1. Context is Important

But first, some context and some general observations about the Voice.

The "Voice" reminds one a lot of the Covid vaccine. Unnecessary. Ineffective. Not fit for purpose. Unargued. Unproven. Experimental. Forced upon us through propaganda and lies. Dangerous. Not the only "solution" to the "problem". Also, much-hyped and pushed, not uncoincidentally, by more or less the very same group of people. Saying "yes" to the Voice proposal is a little like rolling up your sleeve for Australia. No doubt, this is why Pfizer is so cheerily supporting the Voice.

The Voice is also, like so many of the Albanese Government's apparent priorities, a solution looking for a problem. Warren Mundine recently pointed out that there are already over one thousand Aboriginal consultative committees across the nation. An Aboriginal woman recently asked Gary Johns of the "no" campaign, "didn't we do this in 1967?" Indeed. Many of us think that we did.

Then there are all of the various inquiries into Aboriginal matters over the last thirty years. As Gary Johns said in relation to each and every one of these, "Aborigines had a voice. They told their truth". In fact, if you were looking for the real voiceless across the nation, you would not be looking first and foremost at indigenous Australians.[1]

The Voice campaign is a grand opportunity for the in-crowd to virtue signal like never before. It is making the 2017 "love is love" campaign for same sex marriage look tame in comparison. Hence the inevitable appearance of national sporting bodies and "elite athletes", all lining up to just show how hip they are. It is the sine qua non of chances to make your opponents appear deplorable and racist. For my money, this was the reason Anthony Albanese initiated it. Certainly, the political reason.

If the Voice isn't built on the back of popular Indigenous desire, let alone demand, what *is* it built on? The key drivers of the push for the Voice turn out to be guilt, ignorance, ideology, policy-by-emoting, power and narrative. And for at least some, sadly, it is also driven by revenge. About what might be termed "reverse colonialism".

### 2. **Migration and the Aboriginal Question**

There is no doubt that the Voice is divisive. It problematises a largely happy relationship.

But the debate we are forced to be having also creates a false binary of black versus white. It is weirdly divisive. It places front and centre one among many sets of relationships in our largely harmonious society. The Voice is a strange debate to be having in twenty-first century Australia, where now 49 per cent of Australians have at least one parent born overseas. Australia has been driven by the settlement of migrants since 1788. Wave upon wave of new arrivals have descended upon the land with

1 Paul Collits, 'Notes from the No Campaign', *Paul's Newsletter*, 19 May 2023, at https://paulcollits.substack.com/p/notes-from-the-no-campaign.

all sorts of consequences and none of them with the conscious permission of anyone already here. Post-covid, we are expected to accommodate over a million new arrivals in the next two years. What the newer-than-1788 Australians, especially the millions of recent arrivals, make of a black versus white view of their adopted country one can only imagine. Will they, themselves, one day demand justice, a voice and reparations for real or imagined crimes against them?

There can be little doubt that government-directed mass migration and its ultimate purpose, multiculturalism, and the elimination of "whiteness", is (ironically) itself a form of imperialism and of colonialism. Paul Keating famously (if erroneously, in these days of The UniParty) once said, "change the government, and you change the country". Well, how about changing the population? That certainly changes the country. Far more, I would have thought, than simply swapping the political parties in charge.

As Christopher Caldwell put it in his 2009 book *Reflections on the Revolution in Europe*, "can Europe be the same with different people in it?" Can Australia, under the weight of mass immigration? As a nation, Australia has been "changed", over and over. The arrival of the British in 1788 was simply one wave of culture-changing, globally driven migration among many to follow. Each wave has forced profound change on the lives of earlier inhabitants, without their consent. Each wave has been permanent, no less permanent for having been gradual. These waves of migrants combined with the substantial emigration of native Australians over time has altered communities and neighbourhoods in fundamental and irreversible ways.[2]

It turns out that the first Australians are not the only ones to have

---

2 Paul Collits, 'Imperial Globalism, its Forms and Discontents', *Quadrant Magazine*, 11 May 2023, at https://quadrant.org.au/opinion/qed/2023/05/imperial-globalism-its-forms-and-discontents/

had their country removed without their permission.

### 3. Core Questions

At the heart of all of the debates about Aboriginal affairs are two core issues.

One, how do we deal with the legacy of colonialism, whether or not it is regarded as appalling? Should we be guilty? How guilty? Should we remain guilty? What does guilt mean for policy?

And, two, given the fact that Britain settled (invaded?) Australia, what should we do now to address any lingering injustices arising from the Brits' arrival and the ongoing issues relating to standards of living? Or should we forget the history, about which we can now do precious little, and get on with it? Treat all Australians equally. To claim that the Voice will resolve these core issues is to deal in fantasy.

I said at the outset that no one seems to have asked everyday Aborigines about the Voice. If asked to choose between having a debate over what is essentially governance (and power) or a debate over addressing the ongoing, seemingly wicked problems of Aboriginal life, which way would they go? They might well question the question. They might well say that it would have been nice to ask them first.

One of the enduring yet generally unasked questions facing our Indigenous cousins is, are they happy with life in modern Australia, and with their position therein? On one view, you cannot ascribe something like "happiness", or, indeed, its opposite, to a whole people. Yet many often do this very thing. Anyone who advocates for group rights does. Those arguing for the Voice claim that a whole race has been dudded by colonialism. They say that a whole race is searching for lost, stolen meaning. They argue that a whole race wants a voice. This is only one view of what "the question" should be. It is an elitist, top-down view at that.

How would the Indigenous "man in the street" answer the question, individual by individual, "on balance, are you happy or not that the British settled your former continent in the late eighteenth century?" And superimposed a new, ultimately liberal democratic system upon their existing tribal one (I have no need or desire to wade into the terra nullius debate here). I wonder what the majority answer would be. As indicated above, the Maori leaders in New Zealand actually did face this choice, back in the early 1800s. They consciously chose British imperialism over the available alternatives, for rational reasons at the time.

## 4. John Rawls, the "Original Position" and The Voice

Perhaps John Rawls can help here. Rawls made his reputation with his magnum opus, *A Theory of Justice*, published in 1971. Following Rawls, let us speak of the Aborigines' circumstances in 1787 as their "original position". Bear in mind that Rawls saw "justice" in terms of "fairness".

This was the essence of Rawls' "thought experiment":

> *If you could redesign society from scratch, what would it look like?*
>
> *How would you distribute wealth and power?*
>
> *Would you make everyone equal or not? How would you define fairness and equality?*
>
> *And — here's the kicker — what if you had to make those decisions without knowing who you would be in this new society?*[3]

3 'The Fairness Principle: How the Veil of Ignorance Helps Test Fairness', *FS Blog*, at https://fs.blog/veil-ignorance/

To provide a Wikipedia-level summary, Rawls argued that people in a Lockean (after the liberal giant John Locke) state of nature, behind what he called a "veil of ignorance", would choose a particular outcome. They would choose a welfare state. Socialism, if you will. In other words, if we didn't know what our life would be like, we would opt for self-protection rather than leaving our fate to, say, the market place favoured at the time by Rawls' legendary Harvard colleague and sometime philosophical opponent, Robert Nozick.[4] On Rawls' view, we would play it safe. We would choose a system of government that provided for our needs if things went wrong. Rawls was a liberal giant, a storied defender of the big, nanny state. It all rings a bell in this age of safetyism.

The veil of ignorance also provides objectivity about the just society:

> *Philosopher John Rawls suggests that we should imagine we sit behind a veil of ignorance that keeps us from knowing who we are and identifying with our personal circumstances. By being ignorant of our circumstances, we can more objectively consider how societies should operate.*[5]

As a heuristic device, the state of nature has stood the test of time. It is still philosophically respectable. What would we do if we had to take a punt on our life-chances, and what would we demand of our polity? Would we be, dare one say it, "conservative"? It is a little like leaving our baggage at the door, stripping ourselves of our vested interest.

All very interesting, but what does John Rawls' theory of justice have to do with the Aboriginal question (or questions)? It turns

---

4 See Robert Nozick, *Anarchy, State and Utopia* (Basic Books, 1974).

5 'Veil of Ignorance', *Ethics Unwrapped*, at https://ethicsunwrapped.utexas.edu/glossary/veil-of-ignorance#:~:text=Philosopher%20John%20Rawls%20suggests%20that,consider%20how%20societies%20should%20operate.

out that, with a certain tweak, Rawls' "thought experiment" can be very useful. Imagine that an Aborigine in 1787 was presented with two scenarios about life for his people in the twenty-first century. One with a tribal future, another with the trimmings of colonial settlement, refined over time by the granting of equal rights, indeed, privileges, and the rest of the British package. While his own individual position would remain hidden by the veil of ignorance, he would be given a glimpse of two possible futures for his people as a whole. A modified original position, if you will.

Underlying all of these politically crafted agendas lies the core question, what would Aborigines choose in a Lockean/Rawlsian state of nature? Which Aborigines would choose what? If they could have been provided with a template in 1788 for their futures, would they have, like the Maori chiefs in New Zealand, have chosen a pragmatic solution to embrace the Brits and take a chance? In other words, might they have chosen to outsource governance?

Of course, they did not have that choice. But can Rawls' notion of the veil of ignorance give us some clues as to what Aborigines of the day might have chosen? Might they have, shock and horror, have chosen Anglo settlement? The Brits brought innovation, agriculture, democracy, law and order, industrial society, trade opportunities (valued massively by the Maori), and sport. Cricket, Australian Rules Football and Rugby League and Union. Yes, they brought grog and disease too, and all the rest. The colonials may have imposed well-intentioned, time-appropriate policies relating to the welfare of children, that some now feel were "stolen generations". As Nigel Biggar, author of *Colonialism: A Moral Reckoning*,[6] has suggested, British colonialism was a mixed bag.[7]

---

6 Nigel Biggar, *Colonialism: A Moral Reckoning* (HarperCollins, 2023).

7 Nigel Biggar, 'Why History Matters', *London National Conservatism Con-*

Arguably, it was, after all, a beneficial "invasion" by the Brits. It could have been the French, or the Dutch. It was also a benign invasion.[8]

Yes, this is a never-ending debate without end and with zero chance of resolution. But we are where we are. We look at the footy, we see Aboriginal stars doing what they do remarkably well. We see the now much celebrated Indigenous culture, the art, the tourism, the celebrations. Aborigines now have an international brotherhood of Indigenous peoples that is only on offer via the colonialists. None of this would have happened without the "invasion". On balance, what would the First Nations brother (yes, they were sexist, back then, and now) have chosen in 1787, behind the veil of ignorance? I am not equipped to decide. But prominent philosophers like Rawls might just have some insights. Yes, they are white and male...

Rawls' tome was, not without intent, called *A Theory of Justice*. Aboriginal supporters would say, white man's justice, what justice? Yet Rawls was a-racial, as philosophers at their best, are.

Would and should our "personal circumstances" have included race? Would the Aboriginal of 1787, behind the veil of ignorance, have been objective? Yes, I know, objectivity is seen as a white male construct. Like science, religion, and the rest. Whatever. To assert that an Aboriginal in 1787 would not have been capable of liberal-rational decision-making would be, well, blatantly racist. He might even have been enticed by the Western philosophic "trick" of the state of nature device as a means of choosing the good life.

---

*ference,* 17 May 2023, at https://www.youtube.com/watch?v=yRa5Un-ZnK4o

8 Paul Collits, 'The Blessings of a Particularly Benign 'Invasion'', *Quadrant Magazine*, 28 January 2019, at https://quadrant.org.au/opinion/qed/2019/01/the-blessings-of-a-particularly-benign-invasion/

I know what I would have chosen as an Aboriginal in 1787. Is that just me? I would have chosen footy, cricket, the industrial revolution, internal plumbing, advanced medicine, innovation, a moderately democratic polity, moderately free markets, podcasts, video and the rule of law.

## 5. Conclusion

The "Aboriginal question" will never be settled. Let us face this now. It is one of those wicked problems. History is what it is. We cannot go back. But if we could, and we could have had a "Voice to parliament" in 1787, I wonder what the chosen Aboriginal "representatives" of the day would have come up with, way back then. Perhaps they would have opted for the continuation of primitive, tribal society, with all of its familiar comforts and extraordinary challenges, perhaps not.

I remain unconvinced that the Voice to parliament, and the executive, and the truth telling, and the treaty – only one of which is actually mentioned – will enrich our Australian society or, indeed, that of either the 80 per cent of (largely) urban Aborigines that are doing well or of the 20 per cent of (largely) remote Aborigines who continue to struggle. Saying that the "yes" campaign for the Voice doesn't address the "real" Aboriginal problems is true enough. But in this debate between two sides endlessly talking past one another, this isn't the only problem. The larger question is whether Aborigines actually want or need this top-down gift from the elites, and what it will mean for a society that, given everything, is doing pretty well on the race relations front. Without ever before needing a constitutionally mandated and racially determined fourth arm of government.

# 16

# THE VOICE: A LEGAL DECEPTION

**Minny Rozario***

Prime Minister Anthony Albanese announced a referendum question on the proposed Voice to Parliament on 23 March 2023. The Voice encompasses laws which seek to alter the Constitution to 'recognise the First Peoples of Australia by establishing an Aboriginal and Torres Strait Islander Voice.'[1] In brief, it abrogates section 116 of the Constitution and aims to establish pagan animism as priority in a nation that was founded on Christian ethics and democracy.

The premise of the Voice is unjustified as it completely undermines the democratic principles enshrined within the Constitution, as it implies the document is not already set up to value basic privileges such as non-biased suffrage, and the implied constitutional right to political communication.

Secondly, the Voice is being sought after a pandemic which stripped citizens of constitutional rights, indicating its sentiments regarding Indigenous liberties are pure fantasy. As such, this is nothing but virtue signaling designed to paint 'progressives' as

* Minny Rozario is an independent journalist, final year Juris Doctor student and national ministry worker. She worked for seven years in remote Indigenous communities doing scripture-based annual camps.

1 'Voice to Parliament', *Reconciliation Australia,* 2023, at https://www.reconciliation.org.au/reconciliation/support-a-voice-to-parliament/.

'saviours' to the issue of alleged 'race-based inequality', thus garnering votes where they are undeserved.

Thirdly, the Voice is unnecessary given current Indigenous legislation already exists, which offers adequate protections and privileges for Indigenous communities.

Finally, the Voice debate has been politicised in that it is now evident the progressive side of politics is endorsing the referendum as conservatives seek to retain constitutional integrity.

How does one account for this stark divide? It certainly indicates that the issue is more than what it appears at face value. The Voice debate is not about the promotion of greater Indigenous integration in politics at all. In fact, this may spark even greater division within culture. Senator Jacinta Nampijinpa Price is strongly opposed to the Voice, indicating it will force Australians into a treaty which could include reparations, financial settlements, the resolution of land, water and resource issues, and recognition of customary law.[2]

The impending 'treaty' premise would mean Australians face greater GDP taxation and could be forced to pay rates, land tax and royalties to the Voice.[3] For those assuming communistic-style 'land grabs' are mere fantasy, look no further than Western Australia's new cultural heritage laws, which have mainstream media up in arms.[4] The laws will require farmers to pay an Aboriginal consultant up to $160 an hour to do anything on their land which may disturb top layer soil.[5]

2 Gerard Rennick [@senator_rennick]. *Instagram*, 14 June. 2023, at https://www.instagram.com/p/CtdD4clvroD/?hl=en.

3 Ibid.

4 9 News Perth. *Facebook*, 7 June. 2023, at https://www.facebook.com/9NewsPerth/videos/470280258636356.

5 Frank Chung, 'Furious WA farmers fear sweeping new Aboriginal cultural heritage laws will 'hold us to ransom' *News.com*, 15 June 2023, at https://www.news.com.au/finance/economy/australian-economy/furious-wa-farmers-fear-sweeping-new-ab-

Section 5(2)(a)-(b) of the *Aboriginal Cultural Heritage Act 2021* (WA) indicates that Aboriginal people are the custodians of ancestral objects and are entitled to control remains, or secret or sacred items.[6] Remains will likely be found all throughout the WA region, including in suburbs, on farmland and beneath properties. What will happen if remains or sacred items are found underneath schools, staple farming infrastructure or churches? Indigenous animism will prevail to the detriment of all other institutions, departments and infrastructure.

Co-author of *The Voice*, Marcia Langton, has stated the following: "People who are opposing (the voice referendum) are saying we are destroying the fabric of their sacred Constitution. Yes that's right, that's exactly what we're doing." The blatant disregard for Australia's governing legal framework which provides democratic order is apparent within her statement.[7]

The Voice should therefore be vehemently opposed across the political spectrum. It would open up a bevy of legal disputes (flood courts) likely to escalate greater division rather than quell it, and it would disrupt an otherwise foundational document that was set up to provide political, social, economic and cultural stability within Australia to all citizens, on the blatantly false premise of equality.

### 1. Constitutional Principles in Peril

According to law professor George Williams' analysis of the Constitution, there are at least four general doctrines of government which are underlined in it: federalism, the separation of powers,

original-cultural-heritage-laws-will-hold-us-to-ransom/news-story/6886462f8ef6f-2dac076d86a6704cea0.

6 *Aboriginal Cultural Heritage Act 2021* (WA) s 5(2)(a)-(b).

7 Malcolm Roberts [@senatormalcolmroberts]. Instagram, 16 June. 2023, at https://www.instagram.com/p/Cthg60hrD2q/?hl=en.

representative government and responsible government.[8] In order to manifest a system of representative government, Australians must have the ability to "communicate, among themselves, information and opinions about matters relevant to the exercise and discharge of governmental powers and functions on their behalf."[9]

One of the major logical pitfalls of the Voice includes the fact it purports to give greater 'voice' to Indigenous populations. This is antithetical to the Constitution as sections 7 and 24 are indicative of equal political rights to the formation of representative government; a democratic notion which encompasses the fair election of legislative representatives from all cultural, political, religious or social backgrounds.

The right to suffrage for all constitutional citizens is already woven into the matrix of the founding document. An additional 'Voice' from one particular cultural background to the detriment of all others, would completely undermine Australia's democratic integrity. The irony within the entire debate surrounding the Voice is the censorship of conservative platforms which seek to give citizens the reality of the matter. A nation is headed towards dangerous waters of political and social instability when it seeks to amplify certain voices over others and do it all under the false pretense of providing additional democracy, equality and freedoms.

## 2. The Voice Post-pandemic

It is ironic that the Voice is being sought straight after a pandemic which totally undermined Australia's freedoms and democracy. The Northern Territory (NT) for example, was forced into extremely oppressive mandates and strictures, much of which

8 George Williams, *Human Rights Under the Australian Constitution*, (Oxford University Press, 2013).

9 *Nationwide News v Wills* (1992) 177 CLR 1 at 72.

severely impacted Indigenous communities. Where was the Indigenous voice then? It was undermined by the 'equality touting' government ideologues now ironically seeking to change the Constitution for Indigenous benefit.

During the pandemic, the NT had higher vaccination rates amongst the Indigenous community than the national average.[10] The government in the NT claimed this was due to the 'liaison' with Indigenous leaders on the ground. However, research indicates that Indigenous communities are extremely apprehensive of both the medical establishment as well as governing bodies.[11] According to these research investigations, Indigenous leaders 'raised concerns about how COVID-19 information, testing and vaccinations were delivered.'[12] This indicates that many Indigenous people were coerced undemocratically into taking medical experiments which research now indicates, carried serious health risks.[13]

The research also indicates that the Indigenous, frankly, do not hold the government in high esteem. Of course, this is the same government that imposed on Indigenous communities their oppressive mandates, and that is now, patronisingly indicating they need more "voice". Arguably, if the Constitution was being interpreted and applied correctly, the Indigenous should already have a solid democratic voice insofar that any 'necessity' to superimpose additional features would be rendered entirely irrelevant.

---

10 'Interview with Katie Woolf from MIX 104.9 Darwin, on 22 November 2021 on Outbreak in Northern Territory', *Department of Health and Aged Care*, 2023 at https://www.health.gov.au/ministers/the-hon-greg-hunt-mp/media/interview-with-katie-woolf-from-mix-1049-darwin-on-22-november-2021-on-outbreak-in-the-northern-territory.

11 Simon Graham et al., 'Aboriginal peoples' perspectives about COVID-19 vaccines and motivations to seek vaccination: a qualitative study' (2022), 7(7) *BMJ Global Health*, at https://www.ncbi.nlm.nih.gov/pmc/articles/PMC9304971/; Davida Nolan-Isles et al., 'Enablers and Barriers to Accessing Healthcare Services for Aboriginal People in New South Wales' (2021), 18(6) Int J Environ Res Public Health

12 Graham, n. 11.

13 Robert F Kennedy Junior, *The Real Anthony Fauci*, (Skyhorse Publishing, 2021).

### 3. Current Indigenous Legislation

Not only does the Voice undermine sections already existent within the Constitution, but Indigenous agreements and Acts already exist, further testing the appropriateness for a referendum to change the document based on a lie that Indigenous voices do not have a voice within Australia's legal and executive arms.

Naturally, section 127 of the Australian Constitution excluded Indigenous communities from population counts, for constitutional purposes. This provision was abolished following a referendum in 1967.

In tandem with legislative repeals have been the formation of new Acts which sought to reinforce Indigenous rights, post section 127. Two major documents come to mind in light of this: the *Native Title Act 1993* (Cth) and the *Aboriginal and Torres Strait Islander Heritage Protection Act 1984* (Cth). Indigenous voting Acts have already been legislated in Australia's history, for example the *Natives (Citizenship Rights) Act 1944* (WA) has been in place for nearly eight decades.

In addition to these major Acts enshrining the importance of Indigenous inclusivity and existing rights within Australia's democratic frameworks are state Constitutions as well as territory self-government Acts and anti-discrimination laws. Not only are domestic laws encompassing of Indigenous culture and tradition, but at the international legislative level, there is a plethora of human rights provisions, signed by Australia,[14] which undergirds additional strength within Australia's democratic system.

14 *International Covenant on Civil and Political Rights*, opened for signature 19 December 1966, 999 UNTS 171 (entered into force 23 March 1976).

## 4. Concluding Remarks

In light of the above, it is not only fallacious to hold a referendum in order to advance Indigenous 'rights', but such referendum may do a disservice to the democratic framework of Australia. If established, it will ironically give added protections to specified cultural groups on no legally justifiable basis. Rights within legislation is often a balancing act, as competing rights and considerations are juggled in the judicial interpretative process. To change a founding document is no simple task, and referendums often fail as they require full public concord.

There is also something inherently ironic about holding a national consensus to vote on rights for only one specific cultural group in a document which establishes the equality of all citizens before the law. Given section 127 has been repealed and there are now several Acts which enshrine Indigenous rights and considerations within law, it appears that the upcoming Voice referendum will do nothing other than create an unnecessary political divide between the progressive and conservative sides of politics, whilst concomitantly conferring little practical support to the populations it is purporting to empower.

To conclude, empowering susceptible minority communities should be done with common sense and holistic regard for the practical needs of citizens rather than with the drawling promise of additional provisions in a written constitution which was grossly ignored over the past three years. The Voice is therefore nothing but a political trojan horse, which has been orchestrated by progressives to garner votes from the same Indigenous peoples the government behaved so oppressively during the pandemic. If legislators are serious about Australia's democracy, then they ought first to put their language of 'inclusivity and freedoms' into practice and treat existing laws protecting the fundamental rights of Indigenous peoples of Australia with much more care.

# 17

# IT'S BAD: MORALLY, POLITICALLY AND LEGALLY

**James Allan***

Let me begin with a few overall remarks so that readers know exactly where I stand. I am strongly against this proposed constitutional amendment to entrench a Voice body into our Constitution. What is being proposed is in no way at all a modest change. It will go to the heart of our current governing arrangements, in moral, political and in legal terms. The claimed benefits made on behalf of this Voice body are meagre and exiguous. To the extent they exist at all they deal in vague, amorphous symbolism. On the ground, in practice, this Voice body is more likely to lead to bad outcomes, not good ones – for Aborigines as well as the rest of us. It seems likely to me to create a highly political body that deals in rent-seeking, that soon will be seen as a political body by the rest of us, that splits even the Aboriginal community, that soaks up huge amounts of money and demands a purpose-built bureaucracy of its own, that makes passing laws in this country even harder than it already is, and that makes considerably more likely than not

* James Allan is the Garrick Professor of Law at the University of Queensland.

judicial adventurism somewhere down the road. And if I am being totally frank, I would also predict that the positions taken by this Voice body will be those of the activist class, far more often than not positions in accord with the political left in this country, not the right. That might be a benefit to some small section of Australian society. But it will be a pretty big cost to more of us (leave aside the fair likelihood that the lawyerly caste will be net winners should this pass). Oh, and though proponents say it will lead to unity and reconciliation I think it far more likely to lead to disunity, bitterness and a sense that some groups in Australian life get special treatment solely based on birth.

### 1. Moral Problems

The main grievance here is that this amendment will create special rights based on group status. It does not really matter if those special group rights are linked to race (because we can use that term loosely in a way most can follow or we can use it more carefully knowing that 'race' is pretty much a scientifically dubious concept, humans having far less genetic diversity than chimpanzees even) or to some other feature such as 'historical status'. Affording entitlements by group status is simply not in keeping with the bedrock commitments of a liberal democracy and doing so in a country's written constitution entrenches this illiberalism. Indeed, travel down this road flirts with wholesale identity politics. Put differently, unequal citizenship is antithetical to liberal democracy and this Voice proposal takes us some noticeable way down that path. Yes, we have all been told by the Constitutional Expert Group (chaired by the Attorney-General and comprised of nine legal experts, not a single one of whom is a sceptic of this proposed constitutional change) that the Voice will not give Aboriginal people special rights. That, however, is false on its face. A person will have to be within the Aboriginal or

Indigenous constituency to have a say on the membership of this Voice body and, in turn, only that body will have this constitutional power (which I would bet the top judges, in a decade or two, will transmogrify into a constitutional right) to influence Parliament, the Executive government and the public service. No other Australian will have that constitutional power. No other lobby groups; no NGOs; no statutory bodies. Nor will this Voice body be accountable to the vast preponderance of Australians but only to a narrow slice of them, that slice to be determined based solely on characteristics with which they were born. On any Hohfeldian understanding those features amount to a right and as only some Australians will be able to claim it that makes it special. Hence, it most definitely is a special right that this mooted amendment will afford. To repeat, this differentiating of Australians based on group membership (and saying it will not be linked to race but to historical status is a distinction without a difference) is a bad thing. Very bad. And I mean morally bad as well as politically and legally bad. Its consequences are far more likely to be malign than in any way positive.

Here is another moral problem with this whole Voice referendum. The way it is being run looks close to being an attempt to game the outcome or to put a heavy thumb on the scales, most obviously because Labor and the Prime Minister have opted not to fund the 'No' case. Can you imagine what the reaction would have been amongst the great and the good had Mr. Howard decided he would not fund the 'Yes' case for a Republic back in 1999 (when in fact the former Prime Minister back then ran a scrupulously fair referendum in procedural terms)? Now of course the cutesy and near duplicitous response from this government is that 'well, we're not funding either side of the referendum this time, so that's fair'. But this is sophistry. Mr. Albanese knows as well as anyone that the vast preponderance of the corporate, sporting, and even charity world is going to pour money into the coffers of the 'Yes' campaign. One side will have vastly more to spend than the other. And, of course, the ABC and the bulk of the legacy media have a clear preference for one side of this referendum to win and readers do not have to be particularly perceptive to see which side that is. Or to know that this will be reflected in what is reported and how. So withholding government funding from the two sides in this referendum, something that has almost never happened in any of the other 44 constitutional referenda we have held in Australia, goes a long way to making it hard for the 'No' campaign to get its case to the people.

### 2. Political Hazards

Australia already has a comparatively sclerotic law-making process. We are one of only three democracies in the democratic world with an extremely powerful upper house. Canada and Britain, today, have wholly appointed (with, in the latter's case, a tiny hereditary element) upper houses – meaning that they have no legitimacy, no practical veto power and only a limited power to delay proposed legislation. New Zealand has no upper house at all and nor do any of Canada's ten provincial legislatures. Win elections in any of those places and the government can proceed to implement what it promised in its manifesto. In Australia winning an election is nowhere near sufficient. You must also win over the Senate which in practice can mean a handful of Independents or perhaps the Greens. And it will be from that starting point, that in Australia it is already significantly harder for elected governments to implement their manifesto pledges, that the effects of this Voice body will be felt. Because no one thinks democratically elected governments will more easily be able to pass laws once the Voice is in place. The question is simply how much harder, and after how much consultation and cajoling and after how much compromising, will the process be. One might also wonder, given the basic small government v. big government comparative commitments of the two main parties – I speak in general terms you understand, well aware that over the last few years the Liberal party has outspent just about any government going – whether there will be an asymmetry as regards the ease with which left-of-centre and right-of-centre parties will be able to walk this new constraining tightrope of having to seek the input of this Voice body.

My point here, though, is simply that the more this Voice body looks and acts as a sort of *de facto* fourth arm of government, then the harder it will be to enact laws. That may also cash itself out in a calculation that it is better simply to buy off the Voice with more money, to tempt it with rent-seeking, rather than to pick a political fight. Again, the potential risks and costs here strike me as far higher than any perceived benefits.

Let me point to one analogy before moving on to the legal flaws with this Voice proposal. I am a native born Canadian who finished Canadian law school in 1985 just after the *Charter of Rights* had been entrenched into the Canadian constitution. Back then every proponent of this constitutional innovation promised that this instrument would barely affect what were at the time possibly the most interpretively conservative top judges in the common law world. That prediction proved to be completely, and indeed laughably, false. Canada's Supreme Court today surpasses the US Supreme Court in what it is prepared to do in the way of gainsaying the elected legislature. And this is despite a s.33 notwithstanding clause (explicitly inserted to help enable passage of the constitutional amendment) that gives the elected Canadian Parliament great scope, in theory, to over-ride the myriad judicial inroads that the judges have made into social policymaking. So, what about that s.33 over-ride? Well, that legal and constitutional power vested in Parliament has never once been used at the federal level in forty years. Not one single time! You see it proved to be near-on impossible to use politically. And my prediction is that whatever you think of the legal position, that same political reality will play out here in Australia. Political parties of the left will generally like what the Voice body advises. It will not much hamper their agendas. Meanwhile political parties of the right will overwhelmingly lack the will and wherewithal to stand up to it (and those in its corner including the legacy media and bureaucracy and universities). That is the pattern we have seen in Canada and nothing about today's Liberal Party in Australia gives anyone any reason to think things would be different here.

### 3. Legal Flaws

The third sentence of the proposed amendment is unambiguous. The powers of Parliament in this field will be 'subject to this Constitution'. The second sentence of the proposed alteration will be part of the Constitution. I do not see how that does not open the door to myriad legal and constitutional challenges. Parliament's powers will be subject to the Constitution which means (should the 'Yes' vote prevail) that they will be subject to the representations the Voice makes to Parliament. Hence the question becomes whether 'may make representations' (in the second sentence) will be read by a future High Court as a constitutional right to be consulted. I would bet big money that it does, though not immediately. If our High Court in the nominally federalism-related case of *Love* can ground their ratio — when it came to whether a non-citizen person claiming Aboriginal status could be deported — on concepts such as 'otherness', 'deeper truth', 'connection [to Australia that] is spiritual or metaphysical' and more of the same, combining all of those together to claim that judge-made law that purports to speak in the name of the Constitution now recognises 'that Indigenous peoples can and do possess certain rights and duties that are not possessed by, and cannot be possessed by, the non-Indigenous peoples of Australia' and that 'different considerations apply … to … a person of Aboriginal descent', then it hardly seems a stretch to me to think that 'may make representations' will be read as including 'must be consulted'. A decade or two down the road that need for consultation might then, in turn, be deemed to be a basis for invalidating statutes. If Canada is anything to go by the judicial adventurism will not happen immediately. Give it a dozen or a score years. And let me assure readers that the way law schools are today the views of the preponderance of future lawyers (from whom our judges are chosen) will make those of today seem constitutionally conservative in comparison.

And what of the scope of input for this Voice body? Well, that depends on how one reads the second sentence of the proposed wording, in particular 'may make representations to the Parliament and the Executive Government of the Commonwealth *on matters relating to Aboriginal and Torres Strait Islander peoples*'. Would the future draft Bill have to be one that directly affects them? Or not? Because one plain reading is that virtually every single Bill passed by Parliament will in some way or other affect Aboriginal and Torres Strait Islander peoples (as they will the rest of us Australians). Will this new Voice body with the big bureaucracy it will put around itself have a power – perhaps one the judges down the road deem to be a constitutional right – to make representations on just about every policy and every decision that affects Aboriginal people in any way at all? The negative answer can only be along the lines of 'well, our top judges just wouldn't do that'. Yes, and that is precisely the assurance I heard repeatedly back before Canada amended its constitution in 1982, from retired top judges, senior lawyers, and a good number of politicians as it happens. Yet it did happen. Within a half-dozen years, the Canadian judges were even saying that the intentions of those who drafted and ratified the new constitution were, effectively, irrelevant. Relatedly, I doubt very much that future Australian judges will consider any assurances by Mr. Albanese today when construing this new proposed s.129 of our Constitution.

Meanwhile there is this legal aspect that virtually no one on the 'Yes' side mentions. This proposed amendment is to have its own chapter, a new chapter IX, in the Constitution. But putting the amendment in its own chapter – rather than opting not to put it in a separate one – assuredly does not lessen the chances of future judicial activism. It increases the odds and does so noticeably. The Separation of Powers jurisprudence and the implied freedom jurisprudence, directly and indirectly, were founded on the structure and separate-chapters-for-separate-matters nature of our Constitution. I do not see how anyone can confidently predict that this will not be picked up on and used to deliver unknowable innovations in the future. To elaborate on this point, never before in any of this country's previous 44 s.128 referenda has it been proposed to add a whole new chapter to our Constitution. If I were a future top judge intent on 'discovering' or creating some future analogue to the implied freedom jurisprudence I would be sure to make use of this fact.

Those are just a few of the reasons I have for being opposed to this proposed change to our Constitution. And remember this. In the face of uncertainty ought those who live in a country with one of the world's most successful written constitutions throw caution to the wind and take their chances on this amendment for its symbolic value, ignoring the attendant risks of potential future judicial adventurism, identity politics, sclerotic law-making, inroads into the practical ease with which Parliament may act, and the rest? I am a big supporter of democratic decision-making, maybe the biggest in any law school in Australia today. The potential costs here alone, in terms of undercutting democratic decision-making, are very large indeed. Meanwhile the benefits are, well, pretty hard to put your finger on once you leave the realm of nebulous symbolism. So good old-fashioned wariness of this untested and, indeed, of this largely unspecified as to its details, proposal suggests to me that voting 'No' is the wise course of action. The procedurally unfair – verging on the outright gamed – way in which this referendum is being conducted only reinforces that conclusion. It's bad: morally, politically, and legally.

# ABOUT THE EDITORS

**Professor Gabriël A. Moens AM** is Emeritus Professor of Law, The University of Queensland. He served as Pro Vice Chancellor, Dean and Professor of Law, Murdoch University. He also served as Head, Graduate School of Law, The University of Notre Dame Australia; Garrick Professor of Law, The University of Queensland; and Professor of Law, Curtin University. In 1999, Professor Moens received the Australian Award for University Teaching in Law and Legal Studies. In 2003, the Prime Minister of Australia awarded him the Australian Centenary Medal for services to education. He was named the "International Alumnus of the Year" by the Pritzker Law School of Northwestern University, Chicago in 2019. In June 2019 he was appointed a Member of the Order of Australia (AM) for services to the law and higher education. Professor Moens is a *Membre Titulaire*, International Academy of Comparative Law, Paris; a Fellow of the Australian Institute of Management (WA); a Fellow of the College of Law; a Fellow of the Australian Academy of Law; and a Fellow of the Australian Centre for International Commercial Arbitration. He is author/co-author/editor/co-editor of *Foundations of the Australian Legal System: History, Theory and Practice*, LexisNexis, 2023; *Emergency Powers, Covid-19 Restrictions and Mandatory Vaccination: A 'Rule-of-Law' Perspective*, Connor Court Publishing, 2022; *Enduring Ideas*, Connor Court Publishing, 2020; *Law of International Business in Australasia* (2nd ed), The Federation Press, 2019; *The Constitution of the Commonwealth of Australia Annotated* (9th ed), LexisNexis Butterworths, 2016; *Arbitration and Dispute Resolution in the Resources Sector: An Australian Perspective*, Springer, 2015; *Jurisprudence of Liberty* (2nd ed), LexisNexis, 2011; *Commercial Law of the European Union*, Springer, 2010; and *International Trade and Business: Law, Policy and Ethics* (2nd ed), Routledge/Cavendish, 2006. His debut novel *A Twisted Choice*, a thriller exploring the origins of COVID-19, was published in 2020 by Boolarong Press, which also published three short stories, *The Greedy Prospector, The Assistant Librarian's Ambition,* and *The Country Prowler* in an anthology of short stories in 2021, 2022, and 2023. His second novel, *The Coincidence,* was published by Connor Court Publishing in 2021. He writes opinion pieces and commentary for various magazines and newspapers.

**Professor Augusto Zimmermann** is Professor of Law, Head of Law, Chair of the Research Committee, and co-Chair of the Academic Council at Sheridan Institute of Higher Education, Perth. He is also a former Law Reform Commissioner with the Law Reform Commission of Western Australia (2012-2017) and a former Associate Dean (Research) and Postgraduate Research Director at Murdoch University's School of Law. He is also the Founder and President of the Western Australian Legal Theory Association (WALTA), a former Vice-President of the Australasian Society of Legal Philosophy (ASLP), an Elected Fellow at the International Academy for the Study of the Jurisprudence of the Family (IASJF), and Editor-in-Chief of the *Western Australian Jurist* law journal. A prolific writer and the author of numerous articles and academic books, Professor Zimmermann was awarded the 2012 Vice Chancellor's Award for Excellence in Research, and two School Dean's Research Awards, in 2010 and 2011. He served on numerous academic bodies at Murdoch, including: the Research Degree and Scholarships Committee; the Vice Chancellor's Awards and Citations Committee; the Academic Council's Freedom of Speech in Policies and Procedures Advisory Group; and the Academic Staff Promotions Advisory Committee. In January 2015, he was invited by the Tasmanian Chief Justice to address the 'Opening of the Legal Year' in that State. Professor Zimmermann is generally recognised as a fierce advocate for freedom of speech and the Rule of Law, contributing with numerous articles on the subject, including for *The Legal Doctrines of the Rule of Law and the Legal State* (Rechtsstaat) (Springer, 2014), a book edited by the President of the American Bar Association (ABA) that explores the development of both the civil law and the common law conceptions of the Rule of Law. He is the author/co-author/editor/co-editor of numerous academic articles and books, including *Foundations of the Australian Legal System: History, Theory and Practice*, LexisNexis, 2023; *Wokeshevism: Critical Theories and the Tyrant Left*, Connor Court Publishing 2023; *Fundamental Rights in the Age of Covid-19*, Connor Court Publishing, 2021; *No Offence Intended: Why 18C is Wrong*, Connor Court Publishing, 2016; *Christian Foundations of the Common Law* (3 Volumes), Connor Court Publishing, 2018; *Global Perspectives on Subsidiarity*, Springer, 2014; and *Western Legal Theory: History, Concepts and Perspectives*, LexisNexis, 2013. Professor Zimmermann has been included, together with only twelve other Australian academics and policy experts, in 'Policy Experts' – the Heritage Foundation's directory for locating knowledgeable authorities and leading policy institutes actively involved in a broad range of public policy issues, both in the United States and worldwide.